NAVAL COMMAND AND CONTROL

BRASSEY'S SEA POWER: Naval Vessels,
Weapons Systems and Technology
Series, Volume 8

Brassey's Sea Power:
Naval Vessels, Weapons Systems and Technology Series

General Editor: DR G. TILL, Royal Naval College, Greenwich and Department of War Studies, King's College, London

This series, consisting of twelve volumes, aims to explore the impact of modern technology on the size, shape and role of contemporary navies. Using case studies from around the world it explains the principles of naval operations and the functions of naval vessels, aircraft and weapons systems. Each volume is written by an acknowledged expert in a clear, easy-to-understand style and is well illustrated with photographs and diagrams. The series will be invaluable for naval officers under training and also will be of great interest to young professionals and naval enthusiasts.

Volume 1—Modern Sea Power
    DR GEOFFREY TILL

Volume 2—Ships, Submarines and the Sea
    DR P. J. GATES AND N. M. LYNN

Volume 3—Surface Warships: An Introduction to Design Principles
    DR P. J. GATES

Volume 4—Amphibious Operations: The Projection of Sea Power Ashore
    COLONEL M. H. H. EVANS

Volume 5—Naval Electronic Warfare
    DR D. G. KIELY

Volume 6—Naval Surface Weapons
    DR D. G. KIELY

Other series published by Brassey's

Brassey's Land Warfare: New Battlefield Weapons Systems and Technology Series,
    12 Volume Set

General Editor: COLONEL R. G. LEE, OBE

Brassey's Air Power: Aircraft, Weapons Systems and Technology Series,
    12 Volume Set

General Editor: AIR VICE MARSHAL R. A. MASON, CB, CBE, MA, RAF

For full details of titles in the three series, please contact your local Brassey's/Pergamon Office

NAVAL COMMAND AND CONTROL

by

CAPTAIN W. T. T. PAKENHAM, RN

in collaboration with
Dr D. G. Kiely
R. E. Legate
Captain D. Whitehead, RN

Foreword by
Admiral of the Fleet Sir Henry Leach, GCB

BRASSEY'S DEFENCE PUBLISHERS

(a member of the Maxwell Pergamon Publishing Corporation plc)

LONDON · OXFORD · WASHINGTON · NEW YORK
BEIJING · FRANKFURT · SÃO PAULO · SYDNEY · TOKYO · TORONTO

U.K. (Editorial)	Brassey's Defence Publishers Ltd., 24 Gray's Inn Road, London WC1X 8HR, England
(Orders)	Brassey's Defence Publishers Ltd., Headington Hill Hall, Oxford OX3 0BW, England
U.S.A. (Editorial)	Pergamon-Brassey's International Defense Publishers, Inc., 8000 Westpark Drive, Fourth Floor, McLean, Virginia 22102, U.S.A.
(Orders)	Pergamon Press, Inc., Maxwell House, Fairview Park, Elmsford, New York 10523, U.S.A.
PEOPLE'S REPUBLIC OF CHINA	Pergamon Press, Room 4037, Qianmen Hotel, Beijing, People's Republic of China
FEDERAL REPUBLIC OF GERMANY	Pergamon Press GmbH, Hammerweg 6, D-6242 Kronberg, Federal Republic of Germany
BRAZIL	Pergamon Editora Ltda, Rua Eça de Queiros, 346, CEP 04011, Paraiso, São Paulo, Brazil
AUSTRALIA	Pergamon-Brassey's Defence Publishers Pty Ltd., P.O. Box 544, Potts Point, N.S.W. 2011, Australia
JAPAN	Pergamon Press, 5th Floor, Matsuoka Central Building, 1-7-1 Nishishinjuku, Shinjuku-ku, Tokyo 160, Japan
CANADA	Pergamon Press Canada Ltd., Suite No. 271, 253 College Street, Toronto, Ontario, Canada M5T 1R5

First edition 1989

Library of Congress Cataloging in Publication Data
Pakenham, W. T. T.
Naval command and control.
(Brassey's sea power; v. 8)
Includes index.
1. Command and control systems.   I. Title.
II. Series.
VB212.P35   1989   359.3'3041   88–28358

British Library Cataloguing in Publication Data
Pakenham, W. T. T.
Naval command and control.—(Brassey sea
power. Naval vessels weapons systems and
technology series; v. 8).
1. Naval operations. Command & control
I. Title
359.4

ISBN 0–08–034750–9 Hardcover
ISBN 0–08–036254–0 Flexicover

Cover photograph courtesy of *Naval Forces*

Printed in Great Britain by A. Wheaton & Co. Ltd., Exeter

Contents

Foreword

By Admiral of the Fleet Sir Henry Leach, GCB

Two hundred years ago if a government wished to carry out an operation against another power it picked the Force Commander, gave him his instructions and the necessary backing to assemble and equip his Force, and the rest was up to him. Long months later a corvette might bring home a dispatch indicating the outcome of the operation.

Forty years ago if tension became acute it was customary to issue an ultimatum. This specified the action demanded and its deadline, failing which a state of war would be deemed to exist between the countries concerned. Thereafter, subject only to observance of the Geneva Convention, a commander in the field who saw an enemy took him out. The position was clear and unequivocal and the judgement of the man on the spot was paramount.

Today satellite communications provide reliable, secure, near-real-time facilities on a world wide basis, so permitting tight, centralised political control of operations to be conducted through the main shore headquarters with the minimum of delay. Ultimata have been replaced by Rules of Engagement approved by the Government. Furthermore, modern technology enables the mass of information obtained from a wide variety of sensors to be collated, analysed, assessed and displayed in digestible form very quickly. The commander on the spot may therefore no longer be the best informed on the situation. This mass of information, its processing, evaluation, decision-taking and promulgation are all encompassed in the phrase Command and Control—which is what this book is about.

The book sets out in understandable terms the principles underlying the various components which combine to form the complex whole. As an aid to perspective it touches lightly on the past, concentrates on the present and offers a glimpse of the future. And it does so with commendable brevity and lucidity.

Just as, thirty years ago, some Old Hands had difficulty in prizing themselves off their bridge in order to fight their ship more effectively from the Ops Room, so no doubt there will be others today who will growl that they know all about command and control and they don't need a damn book to tell them. They will be equally wrong.

There is a further important point. The book does not cover it, indeed perhaps it could not; but somebody must. The technical facilities described in the ensuing pages involve relevant Cabinet Ministers more directly than ever before in the operational control of the Armed Forces during tension and war. Service officers of the highest rank have long found it necessary to be regularly and personally involved in peacetime exercises. Otherwise they would not be fit to shoulder their responsibilities in real situations. Too often Ministers have been reluctant to do this. From now on they must—nationally and in Alliance terms—or they will not be fit to hold their high office.

This book will be welcomed by professionals as well as those seeking to improve their professionalism; there is scope for all of us to do that.

Preface

As far as I am aware this is the first occasion that all the technical and organisational components of naval command and control have been brought together as one subject. The professional span of the book is thus very wide and I could not have tackled it without help from many sources.

I am most grateful to Admiral of the Fleet Sir Henry Leach for reading the manuscript and for his invaluable suggestions.

I am indebted to David Foxwell, the editor of *Naval Forces*, for permission to use extracts of my articles published in his magazine, which I have drawn on extensively: and also for his help in supplying so many of the plates.

Alan Carnell, Peter Blair and Charles Baker, of Racal Electronics, made many useful comments on technical aspects, and I am very grateful for the time they gave to this.

I am most appreciative of the assistance from those companies who provided information and material. Their names appear in the list of acknowledgements.

Many other people also helped by reading the drafts and commenting on detail, and to these too I offer my grateful thanks.

Finally, I must record my debt of gratitude to my three co-authors, with whom it has been a pleasure to work, and without whose help and co-operation the book could not have been written.

WILLIAM PAKENHAM

Acknowledgements

The assistance received from the following companies or their subsidiaries in supplying information and material used in the preparation of this book is acknowledged with thanks.

British Aerospace
Chemring
Ferranti
Kelvin Hughes
The Marconi Company
Mönch Publishing Group
The Plessey Company
Racal Electronics
Vosper Thornycroft
Westland Helicopters
The Controller, Her Majesty's Stationery Office

CAVEAT

Reference to specific equipments in this book does not imply criticism or commendation of capability or performance.

List of Figures and Tables

Figures

TABLES

List of Plates

List of Abbreviations

ACP	Allied Communications Publication
ADA	Action Data Automaton
ADatP	Allied Data Publication
ADP	Automatic Data Processing
AEW	Airborne Early Warning
AHP	Allied Hydrographic Publication
AIO	Action Information Organisation
AJ	Anti-Jamming
ARPA	Automatic Radar Plotting Aid
AS	Anti-Submarine
ASW	Anti-Submarine Warfare
ATP	Allied Tactical Publication
AWACS	Airborne Warning and Command System
C^3 (also C3)	Command, Control and Communications (spoken, 'C cubed')
CAAIS	Computer Assisted Action Information System
CCIS	Command, Control and Information System
CDS	Combat Direction System
CHOP	Change of Operational Command or Control, as specified
CINC, CinC, C-in-C	Commander-in-Chief
CINCEASTLANT	Commander-in-Chief, Eastern Atlantic
CINCFLEET	Commander-in-Chief Fleet
CINCHAN	Commander-in-Chief, Channel
CIWS	Close In Weapons System
COMINT	Communications Intelligence
COMPLAN	Communications Plan
COMSTRKFLT	Commander Strike Fleet
COMSUBEASTLANT	Commander Submarines Eastern Atlantic
CTE	Commander Task Element
CTF	Commander Task Force
CTG	Commander Task Group
CTU	Commander Task Unit
DCN	Defence Communications Network
DF	Direction Finding

DR	Dead Reckoning
DSCS	Defense Satellite Communications System
DSP	Digital Signal Processing
ECCM	Electronic Counter-Countermeasures
ECM	Electronic Countermeasures
EDC	Error Detection and Correction
EHF	Extremely High Frequency (30 GHz–300 GHz)
ELF	Extremely Low Frequency (0.3 kHz–3 kHz)
ELINT	Electronic Intelligence
ELOS	Extended Line of Sight
EM	Electromagnetic (wave)
EMC	Electromagnetic Compatibility
EMCON	Emission Control
ESM	Electronic Support Measures
EW	Electronic Warfare
FLTSATCOM	Fleet Satellite Communications (System)
FM	Frequency Modulation
FOSM	Flag Officer Submarines
GHz	Gigahertz (= 1,000,000,000 Hertz)
GPS	Global Positioning System
HF	High Frequency (3 MHz–30 MHz)
HFDF	High Frequency Direction Finding
HQ	Headquarters
Hz	Hertz (1 Hertz = 1 cycle)
IFF	Identification Friend or Foe
IMM	International Maritime Mobile (Band)
INMARSAT	International Maritime Satellite (Organisation)
IR	Infra Red
JTIDS	Joint Tactical Information Distribution System
kHz	Kilohertz (= 1,000 Hertz)
LF	Low Frequency (30 kHz–300 kHz)
MAD	Magnetic Anomaly Detection
MF	Medium Frequency (300 kHz–3 MHz)
MHz	Megahertz (= 1,000,000 Hertz)
MNC	Major NATO Commander
MOD	Ministry of Defence
MODEM	Modulator/Demodulator
MRL	Maritime Rear Link

MSC	Major Subordinate Commander
NATO	North Atlantic Treaty Organisation
NICS	NATO Integrated Communications System
NTDS	Naval Tactical Data System
OPCON	Operational Control
OR	Operational Requirement
OTC	Officer in Tactical Command
OTH	Over the Horizon (Radar)
PRR	Pulse Repetition Rate
PSC	Principal Subordinate Commander
R&D	Research and Development
RAF	Royal Air Force
RFA	Royal Fleet Auxiliary
RN	Royal Navy
SACEUR	Supreme Allied Commander Europe
SACLANT	Supreme Allied Commander Atlantic
SHF	Super High Frequency (3 GHz–30 GHz)
SIGINT	Signals Intelligence
SLBM	Submarine Launched Ballistic Missile
SSBN	Submarine, Ballistic (Missile), Nuclear
SSN	Submarine, Nuclear
STANAG	Standardisation Agreement
STANAVFORLANT	Standing Naval Force Atlantic
STUFT	Ship(s) Taken Up From Trade
TE	Task Element
TEWA	Threat Evaluation and Weapon Allocation
TF	Task Force
TG	Task Group
TU	Task Unit
UHF	Ultra High Frequency (300 MHz–3 GHz)
UKMACCS	UK Maritime Coastal Communications System
USN	United States Navy
VDS	Variable Depth Sonar
VDU	Visual Display Unit
VHF	Very High Frequency (30 MHz–300 MHz)
VLF	Very Low Frequency (3 kHz–30 kHz)
WWMCCS	World Wide Military Command and Control System

Glossary

Definitions relevant to Command and Control

Chain of Command. The succession of commanding officers from a superior to a subordinate through which command is exercised.

Command. The authority vested in an individual of the Armed Forces for the direction, coordination and control of military forces.

Command System. The command system is formed by the chain of command and includes the means necessary to distribute orders and to collect, evaluate and disseminate information.

Compatibility. The capability of two or more items or components of equipment or material to exist or function in the same system or environment without mutual interference.

Control. That element of a commander's authority which encompasses the responsibility for implementing orders relating to the execution of operations, all or part of which can be transferred or delegated.

Coordination. The establishment in operations, according to a changing situation, an orderly correlation in time and place of planned actions in order to achieve the best overall result.

Direction. The process of planning, decision making, establishing priorities, formulating policies and imposing decisions.

Full Command. The military authority and responsibility of a superior officer to issue orders to subordinates. It covers every aspect of military operations and administration, and exists only within national services. The term 'command', when used internationally, implies a lesser degree of authority than when it is used in a purely national sense. It follows that no NATO commander has full command over the forces that are assigned to him. This is because nations, when assigning forces to NATO, assign only operational command or operational control (q.v.).

Interoperability. The ability of systems, units or forces to provide and accept services from other systems, units or forces, and to use the services so exchanged to enable them to operate effectively together.

Officer in Tactical Command (OTC). The OTC is the senior officer present eligible to assume command or the officer to whom he has delegated command.

Operational Command. The authority granted to a commander to assign missions or tasks to subordinate commanders, to deploy units, to reassign forces, and to retain or delegate operational and/or tactical control as may be deemed necessary. It does not, of itself, include administrative command or logistical responsibility.

Operational Control. The authority delegated to a commander to direct forces assigned so that the commander may accomplish specific missions or tasks, which are usually limited by function time or location, to deploy units concerned, and to retain or assign tactical control of those units. It does not include the authority to assign separate employment of components of the units concerned. Neither does it, of itself, include administrative or logistic control.

Tactical Command. The authority delegated to a commander to assign tasks to forces under his command for the accomplishment of the mission assigned by higher authority. Tactical command of forces also includes retention or assignment of tactical control.

Tactical Control. The detailed and usually local direction and control of manoeuvres necessary to accomplish missions or tasks assigned.

1

The Naval Command and Control System

A NAVY is an expensive national investment, in terms both of its cost and the resources it employs. Governments only provide and maintain such assets for good reasons: a navy, with its sister services, is an instrument of Government policy, the 'military instrument' as modern parlance has it. Most navies are provided for similar purposes; the deterrence of war, the prosecution of war should deterrence fail, and the protection and advancement of national interests in times of peace. The operations carried out by a navy to achieve these objectives will depend on its size and specialised capabilities. In war, naval operations could include the escorting of convoys, the conduct of anti-submarine warfare, the clearance of mines and the mounting of amphibious operations, to quote only some naval roles. In times of peace, a navy may be required to protect fishing fleets and off-shore resources, to provide deterrent patrols, and to represent the nation diplomatically by 'showing the flag'—again the list is far from exhaustive. The deployment of a navy on such tasks in peace and war involves decision and direction at all levels, from the political and strategic to the operational and tactical; and it generates much activity on the part of naval commanders and their staffs, in ships at sea and in headquarters ashore. The process is known as 'command and control'. Without it a nation's investment in a navy cannot be put to effective use.

The term 'command and control' is an overworked phrase; most people understand what they mean by it—but do not always agree. To some it implies the exercise of command, that is the issuing and execution of orders. To others it is the technical means by which command decisions are made and communicated—the computers, communications and satellites which are sometimes rather confusingly called 'command systems'. In this book the term is used to describe the whole process by which naval forces are subjected to operational direction, and it covers both procedural and technical aspects. We shall therefore be looking not only at the structure and organisation of command and control, but also at the means by which those engaged in it obtain the information they need, how such information is processed, and how instructions are transmitted. This format not only allows the whole system to be studied, it also illustrates the interactions within it; how the requirements for operational control generate technical response in the shape of equipment; how advances in technology offer new facilities and opportunities to commanders; and how, despite such improvements, technical limitations still impose restrictions on operational capabilities and procedures.

The ancient Greeks were reputedly the first to control fleets at sea by the use of flags. Legend has it that at the battle of Salamis in 480 BC the Greek fleet withdrew downwind in good order pursued by the enemy. At the critical moment the Greek commander, Thermistocles, hoisted the flag signal for his fleet to turn and ram. The enemy fleet, dispersed and disorganised by the chase, and caught napping by the unexpected manoeuvre, was defeated piecemeal. This simple story illustrates two of the Principles of War: concentration of force, and the use of surprise. It also demonstrates the elements of successful command and control: a clear chain of command, sound plan of action, an effective method of execution, and reliable communications.

Command Structure

Military Command, to use the official term, is the authority conferred on a superior to issue orders to subordinates. It is usually given legal force, for example by statutes such as The Naval Discipline Act which establish the powers and responsibilities, backed by detailed instructions such as the Queen's Regulations. The application of command in navies is most evident onboard ship or in naval establishments ashore, where the authority of the captain is exercised directly, or by delegation to his officers. However the same principles and powers apply equally at the higher levels.

Command of a naval fleet is based on the organisation of ships into flotillas, squadrons and divisions, which establishes the line of command by rank from the Commander-in-Chief, down through junior admirals to ships' captains. Seniority in each rank stems from the time served in that rank. Thus, when two or more ships meet at sea, it is apparent which captain or admiral is the superior, and who therefore is in command. This system has been in use for many centuries and is still the permanent organisation for administration and everyday occasions. However, since it relies on the grading of rank and seniority it is somewhat inflexible.

For command of naval operations resort is therefore made to two other principles—delegation of command, and temporary command structure. Delegation is a simple matter: the senior officer present (who remains the ultimate superior and who can resume direct command when he chooses) orders a subordinate to take command of a unit, which may be the whole force present, or part of it. The signals ordering and rescinding the arrangement are transmitted to all ships and authorities affected. Delegation of command in this way is used to ensure that tactical command of ships and cooperating aircraft is exercised by the captain or admiral in the best placed or best equipped ship. Transfer of tactical command to the most appropriate officer present is a very normal procedure at sea nowadays; the officer so nominated is known as the 'OTC', or Officer in Tactical Command. Delegation of command and the assignment of ships to lower levels of command is also a regular feature of command procedure at higher echelons, and we shall be looking at this in greater detail below.

Temporary command structures are more complex. They are usually known as

Task Organisations, being designed for use in the execution of particular missions or operations. A Task Organisation is a hierarchy of operational units, usually covering one Task Force (TF) which is then divided and sub-divided into subordinate units. These lower level components are named Task Groups, Task Units, and Task Elements, abbreviated to TG, TU and TE respectively. Each component is logically numbered to indicate its position in the organisation. Figure 1.1, a highly simplified example, illustrates the principles. An important feature of task organisation is that some listed components may be dormant while others are active; ships may therefore find themselves included in more than one component. This allows commanders to reorganise the force using predetermined structures with the minimum of orders and signals. In the example the Surface Action Group, TU 678.1.3 is initially dormant, but may be activated by assigning ships to it from other task units in its task group. This could be ordered by means of a short signal when required—eg if a threat of enemy surface attack develops. The basic rule is that it must be clear, at all times, what components are active and which ships belong to each.

Command in a Task Organisation is straightforward. Each component has its own commander, designated by the unit he commands (eg 'Commander Task Force 678' or 'CTF 678'; 'CTU 678.1.2'), and with a position in the chain of command corresponding to the organisational hierarchy. One individual may

FIGURE 1.1   Illustrative Task Force Organisation

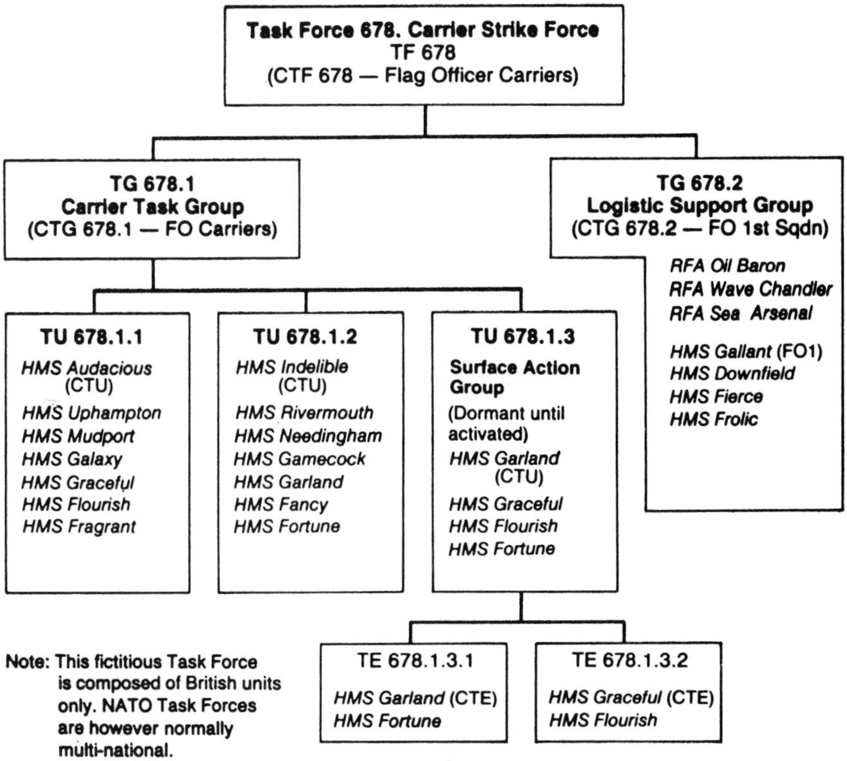

Task Force 678. Carrier Strike Force
TF 678
(CTF 678 — Flag Officer Carriers)

TG 678.1
Carrier Task Group
(CTG 678.1 — FO Carriers)

TG 678.2
Logistic Support Group
(CTG 678.2 — FO 1st Sqdn)

RFA Oil Baron
RFA Wave Chandler
RFA Sea Arsenal

HMS Gallant (FO1)
HMS Downfield
HMS Fierce
HMS Frolic

TU 678.1.1

HMS Audacious (CTU)
HMS Uphampton
HMS Mudport
HMS Galaxy
HMS Graceful
HMS Flourish
HMS Fragrant

TU 678.1.2

HMS Indelible (CTU)
HMS Rivermouth
HMS Needingham
HMS Gamecock
HMS Garland
HMS Fancy
HMS Fortune

TU 678.1.3
Surface Action Group
(Dormant until activated)
HMS Garland (CTU)
HMS Graceful
HMS Flourish
HMS Fortune

TE 678.1.3.1

HMS Garland (CTE)
HMS Fortune

TE 678.1.3.2

HMS Graceful (CTE)
HMS Flourish

Note: This fictitious Task Force is composed of British units only. NATO Task Forces are however normally multi-national.

hold more than one position in the command structure; in Figure 1.1, CTF 678 is also CTG 678.1. Assignment of senior officers to positions of command in a task organisation will usually, but not invariably, conform with their rank. However, once a task organisation is activated by order of a superior, officers are empowered to exercise command in accordance with their position in the structure, whatever their substantive rank and seniority. This allows the most suitable officer to be nominated to the command of each operational unit. Task Organisation is therefore an extremely flexible method of arranging the order of battle for naval operations. It is used for virtually all naval occasions from peacetime Fleet Assemblies to operations of war.

NATO Command

An extra dimension is added to command and control when naval units operate in an allied regime such as NATO. Many nations are involved, each with its own system of military command based on its own laws and defence organisation. However, if the NATO Navies are to work together as one force they must be brought together under a common command structure, accepted and obeyed by all.

NATO is a complex organisation and space allows only a simple description of those features bearing on its command system. The North Atlantic Treaty has the deterrence of war as its principal objective; to this end it provides for exercises in peace, and operations in tension and war, when the resources of member nations—and in particular their 'tactical forces', that is warships, aircraft and army field units—are placed under NATO Command. Such national forces are earmarked and declared in advance as available to NATO at specified degrees of notice and would be assigned to NATO for operational command and control at the appropriate Stages of Alert during a developing crisis. They remain under ultimate national command and may revert to national control if recalled by their national authorities. Most nations retain some forces under the operational control of national commanders; moreover administration and support, and thus logistics, maintenance and repair, are a national responsibility at all times.

The various national units placed under NATO Command constitute a rather heterogeneous force. Although their wartime roles in NATO will have been an important factor in their specification and design, essentially, they are funded and procured to meet national requirements. To provide as much commonality as possible between national systems, NATO pursues an active programme which devises and applies common technical standards, through Standardisation Agreements (STANAGS). These are particularly important for communications and other equipments affecting the ability of tactical units to interoperate. The subject of 'interoperability' and its interaction with command and control is dealt with in a later chapter.

NATO Command Structure takes account of political, geographical and military factors. The geographical area covered by the Treaty is divided into three command areas (Europe, the Atlantic, and the Channel area) and a regional planning area (the Canada–USA region). The three major NATO

PLATE 1.1 AND COVER   A Netherlands naval squadron in close formation, showing the wide variety of aerials and radomes needed for modern naval electronics. (*Courtesy NAVAL FORCES/Audio Visuele Dienst KM*)

Commanders, Supreme Allied Commander Europe (SACEUR), Supreme Allied Commander Atlantic (SACLANT) and Allied Commander-in-Chief Channel (CINCHAN) are responsible to the Military Committee (the highest military authority in NATO) for the development of plans for their areas, the determination of force requirements and the deployment and direction of forces assigned to them. Their command areas are divided into subordinate areas and sub-areas, local geography and national political considerations being important in the delineation of command boundaries and the location of headquarters. Each post in the NATO command structure is designated by rank, and the nationality of the officer to occupy it agreed as part of the NATO process.

Officers of appropriate rank are nominated for the posts by their national authorities, and in many cases 'wear two hats', ie hold both national and NATO appointments. This can be beneficial. In their national hats such officers may administer facilities and command forces earmarked for NATO in an emergency, which will then continue to receive national support. In time of peace they can therefore smooth the process of preparing for the provision of resources required for war. Furthermore, if a chain of national command exists from headquarters down to fighting units, alongside the corresponding NATO command chain, national legal authority applies to orders given and received; this can be crucial for certain orders, particularly those concerning the custody of nuclear weapons. In general, however, officers in NATO appointments issue orders in their 'NATO hat' and these are obeyed without question by their subordinates, since all officers and units under NATO command have been assigned to NATO by the legal orders of their national commanders for the execution of NATO directed tasks. Forces assigned to the major NATO Commanders are usually reassigned by them to the operational control of the appropriate area or sub-area commander, depending on the nature and location of their tasks. Extensive use is made of the Task Organisation system already described, its flexibility suiting it well to the complexity of the NATO command system.

Instructions and Directives

Naval operations come in all shapes and sizes, from the large and complex to the small and routine, often fitting into a pattern in which an overall plan or strategy generates a series of subordinate activities. It is the function of command and control to conceive and plan such operations, and then conduct them. This process involves the promulgation of information and orders, and is accomplished in a number of different ways. Instructions and information of a relatively unchanging nature will be issued in the form of books and manuals—tactical instructions, long-term intelligence summaries, and standardised operational procedures are examples. This body of professional guidance provides much of the doctrine on which other orders and instructions rely for their detailed execution. At the other end of the scale, signal messages, passed to and from ships by radio, provide the means of immediate and real time communication. The ability to transmit signals reliably, securely and rapidly is essential for the conduct of operations. The use of signals for command and control should, however, be reserved for occasions when only a signal will suffice, that is for urgent communication. Letters and written instructions are used whenever possible.

Many naval operations, particularly those which can be foreseen and which require careful coordination of such functions as movements and logistics, must be carefully planned. We shall be looking at how this is done in the following

PLATE 1.2   An American SSBN of the OHIO Class. This nuclear powered submarine is armed with 24 Trident multiple-warhead strategic nuclear missiles, an example of naval capability over which close command and control must be exercised. (*Courtesy NAVAL FORCES*)

paragraphs. However, much naval activity is relatively simple, or alternatively is carried out as an immediate reaction to events. Such operations are conducted on an ad hoc basis. Here the use of signals is essential, backed by the existence of the corpus of common doctrine and standard operating procedures in official publications. This is the procedure which enables a navy to react quickly to such emergencies as disasters and acts of terrorism, and to go about its everyday business with the minimum of fuss and formality.

Larger scale and more deliberate activity involving many ships, some of which may be joining from far away, and complex operations necessitating carefully interlocking movements and coordinated support, will require careful planning and comprehensive instructions. The detailed directions for the mounting and execution of future operations and exercises of this type are therefore issued in the form of written orders, usually referred to as 'Operation Orders'. Such directives are transmitted by secure mail or courier. Promulgating detailed instructions in this way has many advantages. It avoids overloading the radio communications system; the format provides a precise means of conveying a commanders instructions regarding objectives and methods of execution; and ships and subordinate staffs are able to prepare themselves in advance.

The planning process which leads to the writing of an operation order originates, in one way or another, with a political directive. This may take the

PLATE 1.3   A British Type 42 anti-air warfare guided missile destroyer. With her SEASLUG missiles this ship can defend a local area against air attack. (*Courtesy Racal Electronics*)

form of a politically sanctioned general plan such as the NATO Strategy, approved by the North Atlantic Council, or it may be a specific operational directive, for example to recapture the Falkland Islands. Alternatively, operations may originate from contingency plans. These are drawn up to cover eventualities which could occur suddenly (and often unexpectedly), such as the need to evacuate nationals from a trouble spot. In the event of a flare-up, the plan would be ready for a political directive ordering its execution. Whatever the origin, the senior commander or commander-in-chief operationally responsible must decide with his staff how, in military terms, the objective is to be achieved. One of the central issues which will concern him will be the resources—that is the ships, aircraft, support facilities and so forth—to be made available for the mission. Resources are always scarce and it is rare for a commander to be completely satisfied. If necessary, he must be prepared to represent to his superiors that he has insufficient resources for the task and to explain the risks involved if greater provision cannot be made. He will also need to discuss and agree the intended general timetable of events. In all this preliminary work, the commander-in-chief involved will be in close touch with his Ministry of Defence or political headquarters.

Once these basic issues are decided, the staffs concerned can get down to detailed planning and the main operation order can be written. The key element of this is the statement of the aim of the operation. Although this might seem a simple matter it must be given very careful thought, for it guides all that follows. 'The Selection and Maintenance of the Aim' is the most important Principle of

War: long experience has shown that its rigorous application is necessary in order to focus thought and effort on what is really required to be achieved and to avoid effort and resources being diverted to secondary objectives. Statements of aims are particularly important where operations are conceived as an interactive set; each aim must contribute usefully to the whole.

The other main elements of the operation order will be the list of units taking part, the task organisation and command structure, the concept of operations, and the envisaged timescale. Further sections will include the description of the enemy threat, the intelligence background and the communications and logistics plans. However, these are not exclusive; the order will cover all information and guidance that subordinate commanders and ships captains need for its execution. The Operation Order may be issued as one document or, if it is very long, as a Main Order with appendices covering the detail, such as Communications, Intelligence and Logistics. A high level order, such as might be issued by a Task Force Commander, will usually require junior officers in the chain of command (eg CTGs) to issue their own subordinate orders, the format of which will follow similar lines.

However good a plan may be, the success of the resulting operation will depend on how well it is executed. An operation order can be likened to an architect's design, which requires builders and craftsmen to create the building. For this they will use their skills and judgement and apply established techniques and standards. Like the architect, the operational commander plays an important part in directing an operation, but he relies on the coordinated work of many

PLATE 1.4   HMS *Ark Royal* launching a Sea Harrier VSTOL fighter. One of the design requirements for this class of ship was to provide an efficient command and control platform. (*Courtesy NAVAL FORCES. Crown Copyright/RN photograph*)

subordinates for its successful outcome, from his junior commanders and ships captains to middle rank officers and senior ratings. Like the architect, the operational commander can rely on his subordinates to execute his stated intentions in a predictable manner, being guided by a common doctrine based on official guidance, professional training and shared experience. Because this is such a pervasive element of naval life, it is sometimes taken for granted, but without such common doctrine the direction of naval operations would be greatly complicated by the need for extensive instructions on execution. Command and control nevertheless provides the authoritative overlay to many other activities and it is exercised at many levels.

The Chain of Command

At the highest levels, the commander-in-chief maintains close touch with his Ministry of Defence. As we have seen, the MOD issues political directives, states the overall operational objectives, and allocates resources. Within these general guidelines, the C-in-C is responsible for the use of resources under his command to achieve the stated aims, and for the overall direction of operations. Long gone are the days when a commander-in-chief exercised command of his fleet from the flagship. Command at this level is nowadays exercised from ashore, in large, well protected and comprehensively equipped underground headquarters. Unwelcome as this may be to naval officers who would prefer to be afloat, no one today suggests that there is any serious alternative. It is no longer technically feasible to provide the necessary communications, computerised command and intelligence facilities, and staff accommodation, in a fleet flagship, nor would its vulnerability be acceptable. A commander-in-chief will exercise operational command over forces assigned to him by the MOD, transferring or delegating command to subordinate commanders as necessary. The requirement for precise definition of the resulting levels of command, and the need for absolute clarity about what functions and responsibilities are transferred and what are retained, has led to an agreed allied terminology, relevant extracts of which are listed in the Glossary.

In the case of the Royal Navy, Full Command of all operational ships and embarked naval aircraft is vested in the Commander-in-Chief, Fleet. This is the highest level of command, which is never transferred or delegated. C-in-C Fleet may delegate Operational Command, or more usually Operational Control (OPCON), to subordinate admirals, in particular to Area Commanders when ships or units are in their Command Areas, such as those established in the waters around the United Kingdom. Outside these areas, C-in-C Fleet will normally exercise operational control direct. For NATO operations and exercises, Commander-in-Chief Fleet will, in accordance with United Kingdom force declarations, as described above, transfer Operational Command of UK ships and units to the appropriate NATO Supreme Commander; such units remain under his Full Command and can therefore be recalled if necessary. It is however relevant that in his 'NATO hat' C-in-C Fleet is Allied Commander-in-Chief Channel, a Major NATO Commander, and also the Commander-in-Chief Eastern Atlantic, one of the Major Subordinate Commanders under

PLATE 1.5   Royal Navy Sea Harriers in formation. This aircraft proved itself in combat in 1982 during the Falklands Campaign, operating from the carriers HMS *Hermes* and HMS *Invincible* to provide air cover for the Task Force and ground forces ashore. (*Courtesy British Aerospace*)

SACLANT. Moreover his headquarters at Northwood accommodates both his national and NATO staffs. Transfer of operational command of UK units, therefore, usually means that, in practice, they will remain under the direction of the same HQ. Northwood is equipped with a computerised Command, Control and Information System (CCIS) to enable the NATO and UK staffs to handle the heavy flow of information, intelligence and communications traffic involved with the command and control of national and NATO operations.

Whether naval operations are conducted under national or NATO command and control is, generally speaking, exercised at three levels:

▶ *Full Command, Operational Command and Operational Control* will usually be exercised from ashore and will cover the assignment of ships and units to subordinate commanders, the statement of operational aims, the organisation and direction of support (maintenance, logistics and repairs), the processing and dissemination of intelligence and the general direction of operations.

▶   *Tactical Command* of seagoing forces will be exercised at sea from flagships and command vessels. This covers many aspects, the most important of which include the deployment, disposition and manoeuvring of assigned forces, the ordering of states of readiness, and the general direction of operations and warfare in the local area.

▶   *Tactical Control* involves the detailed coordination and control of the force's weapons and aircraft, in furtherance of the orders and directions received as part of the Tactical Command process. It is discussed further in Chapter 7.

Tactical Command and Control

Tactical Command and Control should not be confused with 'Tactics'. The latter are the detailed methods for the optimum use of ships, aircraft and weapons. Tactics are under continuous evolution as new ships and weapons are introduced, and in the light of experience and exercises. It is the function of command and control to decide the correct tactics to use in a given situation, and then to order the appropriate action and supervise its execution. Tactical command and control is therefore dependent, as are all levels of the command and control process, on reliable and flexible communications. The interdependence of Command, Control and Communications was recognised during the 1970s by the coining of the phrase C^3, spoken as 'C Cubed'.

Tactical Command and Control is also dependent on the acquisition of tactical information—obtained both from the force's own sensors and from intelligence sources outside the force—and its processing to provide a complete picture of the local operational situation. From this must be deduced the developing enemy posture and, from that, the correct tactical action. This requires a further set of information, the up-to-date state of available weapons and delivery platforms,

PLATE 1.6   The guided missile cruiser USS *Antietam*, fitted with the AEGIS combat direction system. The plates forming the aerials for her phased array radar are clearly visible on the forward superstructure. (*Courtesy NAVAL FORCES/US DOD*)

such as helicopters and fixed wing aircraft, so that the most appropriate response can be selected. The processing and analysis of all this information, and its presentation in a form which offers a choice of responses, must nowadays be carried out with the use of tactical computers if the answer is to be presented to the command in time for a successful reaction to be initiated. The activity involves many people, from admirals and captains downwards. The process is also dependent on a whole range of modern electronics equipment: radars, sonars, radio positioning systems, satellites, computers with their attendant software and communications systems. During the last decade or so, developments in the technology of this range of electronics have brought about fundamental changes in the manner in which modern fleets are commanded and their aircraft and equipment controlled. The following chapters will describe this equipment and how it is used.

2

The Electro-Magnetic Environment— Above Water Sensors

TACTICAL command and control of naval forces requires two basic elements: information on the local environment, and the ability to communicate information and instructions in the local area. Fortunately for surface ships, these tasks are made relatively simple by the fact that they can receive and transmit electro-magnetic waves with little difficulty. Known also as radio waves, these are the radio frequencies which form the basis of radio communications, radio navigation and radio based sensors and weapons such as radars and jammers. The electro-magnetic (EM) spectrum stretches from Extremely Low Frequencies, with wavelengths of up to hundreds of miles, to X-rays, frequencies with wavelengths of only millionths of an inch. The behaviour varies from band to band within the spectrum, and their different properties are used in a wide variety of ways. Tables 2.1, 2.2 and 2.3 summarise how each band is used typically for naval purposes. Electro-magnetic waves are received and transmitted by electronic equipment and the importance of electronics to modern naval capabilities can hardly be exaggerated. Without this branch of modern technology it would be impossible to mount naval operations of the type and scale now considered normal. We shall be considering in this chapter one main division of naval electronics, above water sensors, with particular reference to their importance to command and control.

Surface ships need to be aware of the position and movement of other ships, aircraft and missiles in the tactical area, in all states of weather and visibility. By far the most important naval surface sensor is radar. Radar is used for warning and surveillance, target tracking and indication, weapon direction, missile control, and for navigation and collision avoidance. Although previous generations of radar, particularly long range warning radar, used lower frequencies, today most ship and aircraft radars operate in the 3-cm and 10-cm bands. Modern technology enables radars employing these frequencies to provide good target discrimination and range, whilst using aerials of reasonable size—important from the point of view of ship design. To use higher frequencies with correspondingly smaller wavelengths, in order to achieve better discrimination or smaller size, would involve using radio bands in which atmospheric effects would begin to have severe effects on range and reliability. Some radars with special

TABLE 2.1

THE RADIO FREQUENCY SPECTRUM
0.3 kHz – 30 MHz

Frequency Band	International Nomenclature (1) (2)		Typical Naval Use	Typical Coverage
0.3 – 3 kHz	ELF	(Band 3)	Submarine Control (Very slow data rate)	Thousands of kilometres (Ground Wave)
3 – 30 kHz	VLF	(Band 4)	Shore to Submarine Communications	0 – 3000 km (Ground Wave)
30 – 300 kHz	LF	(Band 5)	Shore to Ship Communications and Radio Navigation	0 – 1500 km (Ground Wave)
300 – 3000 kHz	MF	(Band 6)	Ship/Shore/Ship Local and Task Force Communications	0–500 km (day) (Ground Wave) 1000 km (night) (Sky Wave)
3 – 30 MHz	HF	(Band 7)	Ship/Shore/Ship Long Range Communications	1500 km (Sky Wave – Single Hop) World Wide (Sky Wave – Multi–Hop)

NOTES

1. ELF = Extremely Low Frequency;   VLF = Very Low Frequency;
   LF = Low Frequency;   MF = Medium Frequency;   HF = High Frequency

2. The Band Number indicates the index of the mean frequency (eg Band 3: mean frequency = 1 kHz = 1000 cycles = 10^3)

requirements may use frequencies in the bands above 3-cm; examples are missile-borne homing radars, where the prime need is to keep equipment small and light; and control radars for Close-In-Weapons-Systems (CIWS), where high tracking accuracy is required over relatively short ranges. These, however, are outside the subject of this book.

Naval shipborne radars can be divided into two main classes; those used to obtain information on the local environment generally, such as surface and air warning, and navigation radars; and those associated with special functions, such as weapons control. In this book we are principally concerned with the first group, which we will call surveillance radars, as these are a primary source of information for command and control. They are also required for the important task of directing friendly aircraft in the vicinity of the force. Surveillance radars scan the local air space and sea surface out to as long a range as practicable. The requirement is for reliable all-weather cover with ranges out to the radar horizon, and ideally beyond. Effective radar range is dependent on a number of factors, including radar performance (which depends amongst other things on frequency band, radiated power and aerial characteristics), and the heights of both the radar aerial and its target. Figure 2.1 shows how the range of the radio horizon varies with height, and Table 2.4 shows typical maximum radar detection ranges. For radar coverage against surface targets the need to mount aerials as high as possible on ships' masts or superstructures is evident. Indeed, one of the most important considerations in ship design is the choice of the highest practicable sites for the aerials of radars and other equipment, to provide the maximum range advantage. Placing heavy equipment high up creates top weight, with attendant problems of ship stability. There are rarely enough good sites for all equipment and so the process inevitably involves compromise.

TABLE 2.2

THE RADIO FREQUENCY SPECTRUM
30.0 MHz – 300 GHz

Frequency Band	International Nomenclature (1)	Typical Naval Use (2)
30 – 300 MHz	VHF	Short range communications, viz:–
		100 – 150 MHz Maritime Air (Air–Ground–Air)
0.3 – 3.0 GHz	UHF	156 – 174 MHz International Maritime Mobile FM Band (Ship–Ship and Ship–Shore–Ship)
		225 – 400 MHz International Military UHF (Intership, Ship–Air, Local)
		200 MHz band Some older air warning radars IFF and D Band radar (see Note 2)
		International Maritime Satellite Comms.
3.0 – 30 GHz	SHF	Centimetric radar (F,G,H,I, J and K Bands) Military SHF Satellite Comms. (7 – 8 GHz)
30 – 300 GHz	EHF	Millimetric radar – weapon control.

NOTES

1. VHF – Very High Frequency;   UHF – Ultra High Frequency;
    SHF – Super High Frequency;   EHF – Extremely High Frequency.

2. For details of the international lettered radar bands see Table 2.3.

The long detection ranges associated with airborne radar are also apparent from Table 2.4, which explains the advantages of maritime air reconnaissance, and of specially equipped aircraft like AWACS. Note also the corollary; high flying aircraft can be detected at long range, which makes a lower level approach essential if this is to be avoided. The sea skimmer missile is the ultimate example of this ploy.

The maximum ranges in Table 2.4 assume normal propagation conditions. In

TABLE 2.3

INTERNATIONAL LETTERED FREQUENCY BAND DESIGNATIONS

Band Edge Frequency	Band Designation	
	Current	*Previous*
1.0 GHz	D	L
2.0 GHz		
	E	
3.0 GHz		S
	F	
4.0 GHz		
	G	
6.0 GHz		C
	H	
8.0 GHz		
	I	
10.0 GHz		X
	J	
20.0 GHz		K
	K	
40.0 GHz		
	L	
60.0 GHz		Millimetric
	M	
100.0 GHz		

FIGURE 2.1   Radio Horizon Range

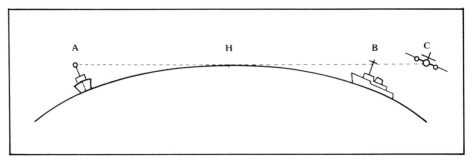

Radio Horizon range for:
Ship "A" is AH
Ship "B" is BH
Aircraft "C" is CH
given by the approximate formula RHR = (1.125 × √h) miles
where h = height above sea level in feet.

Under normal propagation conditions, maximum radar detection range
(and maximum range of line-of-sight communication) is the sum of the radio
horizon ranges of the transmitter aerial and the target (or receiver).

Thus maximum radar detection range of Ship "A" from:–
Ship "B" is AH + BH = AB
Aircraft "C" is AH + CH = AC

this state radar beams travel in straight lines and the geometry of Figure 2.1 applies. However, in settled conditions, particularly during hot weather, the temperature and humidity of the air do not reduce steadily with height in normal fashion. Temperature inversions, layers and ducts are formed which may cause radar beams to be refracted and thus 'bounced' back to the surface again, where further reflection off the sea may cause the process to be repeated. This is termed anomalous propagation or 'anaprop', and can lead to radar waves travelling perhaps up to hundreds of miles further than normal. The process is very similar to the effect on sonar of temperature layering of the sea, which is discussed in a later chapter, and it also affects other uses of EM waves at frequencies above 30 MHz, such as line-of-sight radio communications. The effect is unpredictable, and is therefore difficult to exploit. The main result is to cause interference on radar displays, and to make it unsafe to rely on the range of normal propagation being the only distance at which an enemy can intercept one's transmissions.

Nowadays, naval radars are very reliable, particularly when they use one of the many signal processing techniques now available for enhancement of the wanted echo, the suppression of sea clutter and the elimination of false echoes, such as clouds. Software controlled digital processing can further refine the output before being passed to the computer system; for example, an initial assessment may be made of target characteristics, and target radial velocity measured, using doppler methods. The virtual disappearance of raw (ie unprocessed) radar data presented for human or computer consideration is an important development in radar technology, providing greatly improved infor-

TABLE 2.4

TYPICAL MAXIMUM RADAR DETECTION RANGES
(in miles)

RADAR PLATFORM		TARGET			
		Carrier	Frigate	Bomber	AEW Aircraft
	Height	100 ft	50 ft	40,000 ft	5,000 ft
Carrier	100 ft	22	19	211	81
Frigate	50 ft	19	16	208	78
Bomber	40,000 ft	211	208	N/A (Note 2)	N/A (Note 2)
AEW Aircraft	5,000 ft	81	78	270	140

Notes.

1. These figures assume normal propagation conditions.

2. Bomber's radar would probably lack sufficient power to detect other aircraft at extreme range.

mation. Another powerful technique is to operate the radar automatically under digital control, and then harness it to the computerised command system. These examples of the use of signal processing and computer control illustrates the degree to which command and control is now affected by software in virtually every activity. We shall be returning to this subject and its implications throughout the remainder of the book.

Shipborne Surveillance Radar

With shipborne centimetric radars, a target, when detected, is fed into the ship's command system. Here it is compared and correlated with other information, obtained either from other sensors on that ship or from outside sources, passed in by radio or data link. The detection is then plotted to develop a track and confirmation obtained that it is indeed a new target and not a further detection of an existing track. Most importantly, the new track is assessed as soon as possible to establish whether it is friendly or hostile. This assessment is based partly on the target's tactical behaviour (for example, whether it is closing in a menacing manner) and partly on other sources of information such as IFF or ESM, which we will be examining in later paragraphs. Modern radar displays use colour to distinguish between different categories of target and to highlight differing classes of information. The tactical decisions which result from the display and analysis of this information, and subsequent action, such as the selection of an appropriate weapons response, are described in Chapter 6. We should however note that the information from the radar, being in digital form, can be passed not only to the computer command system but also direct to the appropriate target indication radar, which will acquire the track and indicate it to the selected weapons control radar. Handling radar information in this way allows an automatic weapons response to be initiated against very fast moving threats such as sea skimming missiles. This is also explained in Chapter 6.

Surveillance radars must scan in azimuth with narrow horizontal beamwidths, typically of 1° or so, in order to discriminate between close targets. For many years the beam of air warning radars was approximately fan shaped, that is it extended upwards in a thin wedge so that it would detect both low flying and high flying aircraft on the same bearing. To provide accurate height it was necessary to use an additional height-finding radar, with a pencil shaped beam; this would train to the correct azimuth and then search in elevation for the wanted target. The angle of elevation thus obtained, when combined with range, yields height. However, this procedure is too slow for modern needs, with aircraft and missiles capable of hitting naval targets within a few seconds of first detection. Instantaneous knowledge of azimuth, range and height is required by the ship in order to permit an effective response. Two different types of radar have been developed for the purpose, both known as 'three dimensional' or 3-D radar. The first, an example of which is the British Type 996, manufactured by Plessey, uses mechanically rotated aerials to obtain azimuth, but the vertical fan is effectively made up of a number of pencil beams, enabling immediate measurement of height. A more sophisticated type, known as a phased array radar, uses beams that are shaped and scanned electronically in both the horizontal and vertical dimension. The aerials are large flat arrays, probably integrated with the superstructure, as they are too heavy to mount up a mast. The radar associated with the United States Navy AEGIS system is an example. At present, such radars are too big and expensive to be fitted other than in larger warships, although developments to provide smaller versions are expected.

To obtain an ability to see beyond the horizon, which is not possible with centimetric techniques, a special type of radar using HF surface wave may be employed. An HF surface wave is to some extent guided by the sea surface and so can be used to propagate around the earth's curvature and cause a return echo, as with conventional radar. Such radars may be deployed as bi-static systems, with high power transmissions from transmitters based on shore, with receivers and displays in ships utilising the resulting echoes. The advantages of this method are that much higher power may be used than would be practicable from a ship,

PLATE 2.1   The aerial system of the Royal Navy Type 996 3-D radar. (*Courtesy Plessey*)

and the fact that the ship, by not transmitting, avoids radiating HF signals which, as we shall see in a later chapter, are easily detectable and reveal the ship's position to an enemy. HF radars of this type will detect ships and low flying aircraft below the lobe of centimetric radars. Compared with conventional radars they lack precision and definition, but their over-the-horizon (OTH) capability is important.

Of course, not all shipborne surveillance radars are as large or as complex as these examples. Smaller craft require smaller and less costly equipment. Although the performance is inevitably lower than the major systems described, such craft do not have need of an extreme capability. An interesting example, suitable for patrol craft or corvettes is provided by the Racal 2459 F/I radar, which provides combined air and surface warning, with an ability to direct helicopters, and a discrimination good enough to enable it to be used as a navigation radar as well. The saving in cost and topweight by meeting all these needs in one equipment is attractive in small vessels. In the example quoted it is made possible by using two radar frequencies. The air warning capability is provided using F Band, while the surface and navigation components use I Band, both integrated into a combined display.

PLATE 2.2　The Netherlands naval auxiliary *Poolster* replenishing at sea. The twin element aerial of her 2459 F/I radar is mounted on the platform above the bridge. (*Courtesy Racal Electronics*)

Airborne Radar

Airborne radar is another important branch of the discipline. In fact electronics are, if anything, more important to aircraft than ships. The cockpit and controls of modern fixed wing aircraft and helicopters are designed around the electronics suite. Aircraft have specialist radars to assist them with mission tasks, such as the effecting of interceptions and the control of airborne weapons, and to give warning of enemy homing missiles. Such radars however are outside our subject. What we are concerned with is airborne surveillance radars for reconnaissance, and airborne early warning (AEW)—radars which are used to extend the range of information available to ships. The aircraft may be shore-based and cooperating with ships at sea, carrier-borne, or, in the case of helicopters, organic to surface warships and naval auxiliaries.

PLATE 2.3   A French Atlantique maritime patrol aircraft. Her main radome shows below the fuselage. (*Courtesy NAVAL FORCES/Verlaqsgruppe Mönch*)

The main technical challenge behind aircraft radar, indeed to airborne electronics in general, is to design equipment which is small and light enough for carriage in aircraft yet robust enough to provide reliable service in a demanding environment, and with a sufficiently high performance for the task. In the case of long range radar, one of the main problems is to provide enough power. Here modern techniques of clutter suppression, echo enhancement and signal processing are especially valuable tools, since they offer a means of improving the signal-to-noise ratio, and thus maximum detection range, without commensurate increase in output power. Another problem is the size and shape of the aerials. Using conventional techniques there is no way of avoiding the need for an aerial of sufficient width to provide adequate sensitivity and discrimination, as can be seen from the odd-looking aerials on many aircraft equipped for long range surveillance.

PLATE 2.4   A US Navy E2C HAWKEYE AEW aircraft takes off from its parent carrier, showing its piggyback mushroom radome. (*Courtesy NAVAL FORCES*)

There is an interesting variant in radar techniques known as 'synthetic aperture', made possible by digital processing. Here the aircraft flies across the phase front (ie at right angles to the required direction of coverage) and precisely timed radar signals obtained. These are then correlated and processed under computer control to recover a synchronised picture, which approximates to the definition and gain that would be obtained from an aerial of very long length. Despite its apparent advantages, this type of radar is awkward to use operationally, and is not common. However, whatever type of radar may be fitted, because of the height at which aircraft can fly, coupled with the ability to deploy them on reconnaissance and patrol hundreds of miles from the force, maritime air reconnaissance and airborne early warning provide a force commander with invaluable tactical intelligence at ranges far in excess of those obtainable from ship radars.

The operational importance of extending force radar coverage beyond the restricted confines imposed by the radar horizon was demonstrated in dramatic terms during the Falklands Campaign. With the demise of the carrier-borne AEW GANNET aircraft, the Task Force, which, of course, was operating thousands of miles beyond the range of friendly shore based AEW, was unable to obtain adequate warning of the approach of missile-armed enemy aircraft. Urgent ad hoc measures were taken in the UK to re-package existing suitable radars so that they could be deployed as extempore AEW radars slung under helicopters. These gave all-round radar cover and, despite the vulnerability and limited endurance of the helicopters, confirmed the value of organic carrier-borne airborne early warning.

Navigation Radar

Discussion of surveillance radars would be incomplete without consideration of the use of radar for navigation. Like other surveillance radars, such equipments

PLATE 2.5 An AEW variant of the SEA KING helicopter, fitted with the THORN-EMI SEARCHWATER marine surveillance radar. This version of the SEA KING was developed as a result of operational experience during the Falklands Campaign. (*Courtesy Westland Helicopters*)

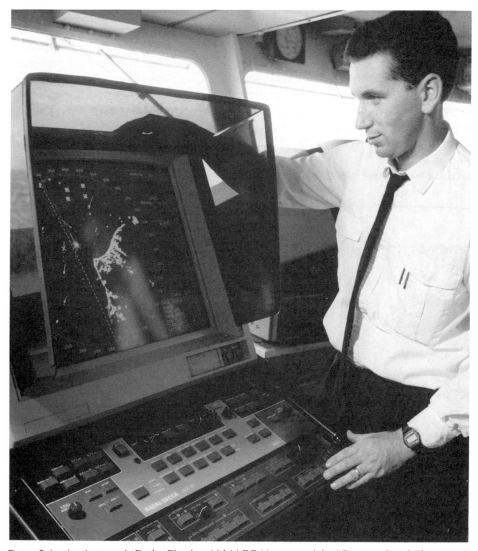

PLATE 2.6   An Automatic Radar Plotting Aid (ARPA) on sea trials. (*Courtesy Racal Electronics*)

are all-round looking, and give warning of surface targets. However, their characteristics are optimised to provide good coverage of such features as land, visible rocks and lighthouses and small targets, such as navigation buoys. They are designed to give highly accurate range and bearing and excellent discrimination between close echoes, together with the ability to operate successfully down to very close ranges, thus enabling ships to navigate around such hazards as exposed rocks and breakwaters. To achieve these characteristics, the extreme warning range of other types of surveillance radar is sacrificed. Naval navigation radars are usually based on civil equipment, as the navigational tasks are very similar to those in merchant ships. Such radars are frequently connected to an Automatic Radar Plotting Aid (ARPA), a console which displays the surface picture and provides a number of controls and facilities which assist the mariner. These may include automatic tracking of radar targets, vector analysis aids to assist rendezvous or collision avoidance and warning devices to give visual or sound indication of hazards, such as ships on collision bearings and the dragging of the ship's anchor. A typical naval navigation radar, used by the Royal Navy, is the Type 1007, designed by the manufacturer, Kelvin Hughes, building on the technology of its civil radars for merchant ships. The importance of such radar to command and control is that it enables warships to be navigated at night and in low visibility in safety, even when operating in groups in close formation. It also allows the captain, (who, in former years was confined to the bridge for the sake of ship safety), to see for himself what is going on and to move, when required, to the ship's Operations Room, leaving an experienced officer on the bridge. The captain in the Ops Room has the use of the navigation monitor display and thus

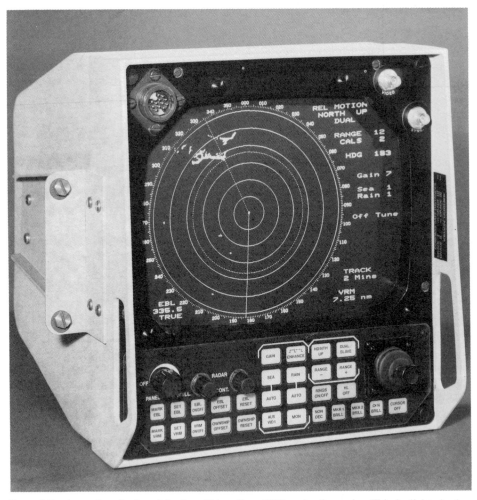

PLATE 2.7   A monitor display of the Royal Navy Type 1007 navigation radar. This daylight-viewing portable monitor is normally fixed, but may be moved if required. (*Courtesy Kelvin Hughes*)

has the same view of the radar as those on the bridge. In an emergency, he can move to the bridge to take charge. We shall see in a later chapter that the ability of the captain to direct the fighting capability of the ship from the Ops Room is an important feature of modern naval warfare.

ESM—the Passive Mode

Before leaving the subject of radar, mention must be made of the use of the passive mode to analyse radar signals transmitted by the target, rather than a return echo. In practice, such receivers are specialist equipments designed to be used to intercept all forms of radio signal within their frequency range, not just radar signals; for example, many communications and radio-navigation services operate at frequencies in similar parts of the frequency spectrum. Organisationally, the subject is a branch of Electronic Warfare, known as Electronic Support Measures (ESM), and is dealt with fully in the next chapter. It requires some treatment here, however, since the information available from ESM provides a most valuable adjunct to that available from radar alone. In fact, after radar, ESM is the most important source of tactical information. ESM provides the command with two types of information not available from other methods. First, it gives the earliest definite warning of the presence or approach of an enemy, since a transmitting radar can be detected by its intended target using an ESM receiver at considerably greater range than it will itself detect that target. Second, because ESM can provide an electronic signature of all emitters on the target platform, it provides a far better assessment of platform identity than radar alone.

IFF

Another means of obtaining identity of a radar echo is provided by a type of coded secondary radar known as 'IFF'; this is an abbreviation for 'identification, friend or foe', and the system was developed in World War II to enable air defences to distinguish friendly fighters from hostile bombers. Although usable by ships, its principal application is in aircraft and the following description refers to aircraft use.

IFF equipment is usually associated with a radar, operating on different frequencies but effectively integrated with, the radar for control and display purposes. It transmits signals which cause IFF transponders to transmit a coded signal in response. Such transponders are, of course, fitted in friendly units. But they could be copied and fitted by the enemy too. Thus it is essential that the system is cryptographically protected to ensure that only friendly units respond. There are a number of available codes, which can be used, in several ways, to pass information on the identity, state or operational role of the responding unit. In the ship, the response is received in the IFF receiver and, after being decoded, is displayed on the associated radar display. Here it is correlated with the aircraft radar track. As well as an immediate indication of whether the track is friendly, IFF therefore provides other valuable tactical information on its identity. Aircrew can select and change the code in use, and this facility can be used in various ways to enhance the ship's understanding of the situation and to pass simple information, such as a change of state in the aircraft. In addition, the indication of the IFF response on the radar display, just behind the real echo, may show up better than the radar echo itself. This can be very useful for the direction of friendly aircraft in marginal conditions, such as extreme range, heavy rain or enemy jamming.

There is an important practical difficulty. If IFF is in use, friendly aircraft not equipped with it are, of course, in great danger of being treated as hostile. Thus, for IFF to be fully effective, all nations of the Alliance must implement the system and all operational units in a particular scenario must carry and use the equipment. Current IFF systems are obsolescent and NATO has had an Operational Requirement for a modern system for several years. Only when this has been designed and introduced will the full potential of the technique be realised.

Radio Navigation

Radar and IFF were children of World War II, developed under the pressure of operational need to provide new and more effective methods of combating air attack. It is sometimes forgotten that the use of radio for aeronautical navigation was an even earlier invention, providing an aid for instrument landing in the 1930s; this was further developed during the war to provide a navigation system for guiding bombers to their targets. The techniques of radio navigation are now widespread and are standard to all forms of civil and military air operations; they also cover the oceans, and look like spreading into use over land for mobiles such as taxis and trucks. The basic techniques have also themselves become specialised. In addition to the original purpose of enabling an aircraft or ship to know its position, there are now similar radio systems for airfield approach and landing, radio beacons and highly accurate systems to provide the precision needed for surveying and positional control. Many of these applications are important elements of modern naval capability. For example, in the case of ballistic missile firing submarines, knowledge of the vessel's precise position is essential to the accuracy of the weapon system.

Radio navigation systems are mostly passive in nature, that is to say, they operate on the basis that the user platform which requires the information must receive and analyse signals from external sources. Nowadays, systems are divided into two main divisions, terrestrial and space-based. The original systems of WWII were of course terrestrial and the well-known DECCA Chains were introduced for general marine use shortly after. Systems such as DECCA, LORAN 'C' and OMEGA are known as hyperbolic systems; they work on the basis that the equipment onboard measures the difference of time of arrival (TD) of a pair of signals from two known shore transmitters, known as the Master and Slave Stations. The value of TD places the position of the ship on a line (mathematically a hyperbola); a second pair of signals yields another, and intersecting, hyperbola which fixes the ship's position uniquely. Each master station is associated with three or more slave stations. Known as a chain, they are geographically sited to give coverage of the required ocean area. DECCA and

PLATE 2.8   Radio Navigation Receivers and Displays. A typical Satnav receiver in the foreground, with a DECCA Mk 21 Navigator behind. The ship's position can be read directly from such displays. (*Courtesy Racal Electronics*)

LORAN 'C' operate in the Low Frequency Band and are essentially coastal systems. OMEGA operates in the Very Low Frequency Band and provides ocean coverage. The positional accuracy of such systems is typically about 0.5 miles or better, depending on range from the shore and angles of cut. LORAN

'C' also operates on a different technical principle known as range-range—or 'rho-rho'—which requires the ship to be able to have a very accurate time reference. In this mode, position may be accurate to about 100 metres. HYPER-FIX is a refined version of the DECCA system, which is in use around the coasts of the UK to provide 10–20 metres repeatable accuracy, ie a ship can return to a position with that degree of confidence. Such systems are invaluable for mine-countermeasures use, as known or suspected mines can be pinpointed and either removed or avoided.

Space-based navigation aids have been in use since the 1960s, when the SATNAV TRANSIT system was introduced by the Americans as part of their POLARIS programme. A number of satellites are maintained in relatively low polar orbits, with periods of the order of hours, and organised so that the ship or submarine has a choice of several. The system operates on the principle that the position and track of each satellite is known with great precision, and measurement of the doppler of the selected satellite during a pass gives two possible positions, one of which is discarded by reference to the vessel's dead reckoning position, or DR. As the time of each satellite's passage overhead is known from published tables, this system allows submarines to come to periscope depth for the observation for the minimum time, which is important to submarines, as we shall see later. The accuracy of TRANSIT varies with geographical position and the parameters of the satellite in use, but accuracies better than half a mile are obtainable. The best value can be obtained by using this system in conjunction with another, such as OMEGA, and the submarine's own inertial navigation system.

Inertial navigation systems are the exception to the general rule that electronic navigation aids require external signals for their operation. They exploit the properties of gyroscopes and accelerometers to determine where the ship or submarine has moved to, from a known point. Mechanical gyros are currently employed in ships, although cheaper equipment of comparable accuracy, using ring-lasers, will shortly come into service. The main application of inertial navigation systems is in submarines, particularly nuclear powered ones, which are of course normally cut off from radio navigation reception when submerged. The vessel obtains an accurate radio fix before diving and thereafter when opportunity offers. Whilst submerged it uses its inertial system to run on its dead reckoning, which, in this case, is highly accurate. Surface ships may also use inertial systems to provide positional updating between radio fixes and to cover for periods when the radio system may not be available (eg in war). The period for which an inertial system will remain within the required limits of accuracy, before needing an updated position obtained externally, may therefore be as important a feature of its specification as its intrinsic accuracy.

Navigation systems are important to command and control for three principal reasons. The first we have already discussed, namely the ability to position a ship, or more likely a submarine, extremely accurately in order to provide the reference point for weapon delivery. Secondly, and perhaps more obviously, they enable ships and aircraft to be navigated safely in conditions when visual navigation may be impossible, and often to much higher degrees of positional accuracy. Thirdly, they are the basis on which ships and aircraft report contacts.

The position of a radar echo, detected, say, 15 miles due north of a ship or maritime aircraft, is only meaningful to other ships, or authorities ashore, if the position of the platform itself is also known precisely. At present, as we have seen, ships know their positions in ocean areas to varying degrees of accuracy, depending on what navigational aids are available but, in general terms, this will be of the order of, say, one nautical mile. Whilst this is sufficiently accurate for general surveillance and reporting, it leaves room for confusion in a battle situation, when enemy contacts, for example in an incoming raid, may be dense. One aircraft reported by two ships may appear to be two contacts unless the positions of the reporting vessels are known to a high degree of accuracy. Far greater confusion can occur with a raid by several aircraft reported by several ships, and it will be impossible to separate their tracks and decide how many aircraft are present unless the ships' positions are known to a higher level of accuracy than the distance by which the aircraft themselves are separated. An important branch of this tactical use of highly accurate navigational information is mine-countermeasures or MCM. The difficulty of sweeping or clearing modern mines is such that it may be preferable to hunt them, that is to detect mines or suspected mines and then return to identify and destroy them. Alternatively, their position may be reported and ships may navigate safely around them. The need for highly accurate radio-position systems for this work is self evident.

For all these reasons, probably one of the most significant additions to command and control capabilities will be introduced during the next decade. This is the Global Positioning System (GPS), the remarkable American satellite-based radio navigation system now undergoing operational trials. GPS, when fully deployed, will use a constellation of 18 satellites with three operational spares, in orbits designed for world-wide coverage. Each satellite transmits, using spread spectrum techniques, a unique digitally coded radio signal, which includes its own reference correction data, which identifies its exact position. GPS operates on the principle that each user receives such signals from the three or four best placed satellites, his specialised receiving equipment measuring the difference in their times of arrival. This enables the user platform's position and velocity to be established in three dimensions, as well as a precise time reference. The system will therefore give aircraft height as well as ships' positions. The accuracy is higher than any long range system in service now, and will be typically of the order of 100 metres or better, with time reference information to match. For naval use, an extra channel of encrypted information provides accuracies of the order of ten metres or so, available to units with the associated receiving and decoding equipment. GPS will enter service with the United States Armed Forces during the 1990s and also with the Royal Navy and RAF, NATO and several Commonwealth countries. It will provide a common world-wide position and time grid, enabling not only the reporting of contacts to hitherto unthought of degrees of accuracy, but also the provision of the basis for accurate weapon coordination, for which precise time reference is becoming essential. It seems certain that once GPS is established across the fleets of NATO it will provide a means of tactical cooperation on a scale not possible today.

It is worth noting the ability to provide the relative positions of ships and aircraft within a force provided that they are participating in a modern data link. This facility is available with Link 16, due to be introduced into NATO and other navies in the next few years, and discussed in Chapter 5. The separation between units is obtained by accurate timing of their transmissions and this yields the relative positions of all units when resolved in the computer. It then only requires one unit to be receiving GPS to give all units the same degree of absolute accuracy.

Although not a radio navigation equipment, mention should be made of the 'electronic chart', which is of growing interest and importance. This device uses components very similar to the familiar television video recorder and personal computer. The information drawn on a conventional chart is recorded instead on a video disc which, for use by the mariner, is displayed on a colour VDU, with keyboard and cursor controls. The ship's position is shown, obtained from its own navigation sensors, or manually inserted from visual fixes, and run on as a DR position from its helm and log readings. All information normally available, such as coastlines, depths, navigation marks and features such as lighthouses and rocks, are, of course, shown. The ship's future position, calculated from the set course and speed, may also be displayed. To this, vector analysis may be applied automatically to take account of the effects of tide and wind. The scale of the display may be adjusted to show a whole ocean for route planning, the medium range display required for coastal navigation, or the fine detail and short range needed for movement in harbours. Not least of the advantages of these devices is the ease and speed with which the charts may be up-dated to show new hazards— a simple keyboard operation inserting new or replacement information, instead of the laborious and messy pen and ink corrections needed for traditional charts. These developments represent the application of information technology to the traditional art of navigation, and development is aimed at the large civil marine market. However, there will certainly be important advantages to navies; to list only one naval application, consider how much simpler it will be to navigate along swept routes (the mine-free channels established in war) using such devices.

Satellite Surveillance

Before leaving the subject of above water sensors, mention must be made of the use of satellites for surveillance. Satellites are, of course, platforms hundreds of miles high in the sky. As surveillance systems they are only as good as the equipment they carry as payload. In this connection, they suffer from several fundamental disadvantages, the first of which is that the size and weight of the equipment they can carry will be severely restricted compared with what might ideally be specified for terrestrial systems. Aerials and their parent equipment are likely to be much smaller and lighter in satellites than their designers would prefer. Another current limitation is likely to be electrical power, which, with existing technology, cannot be made available in quantity in space. These restrictions at present make the use of active radar as a satellite sensor less attractive than might be supposed, although there are indications that they may eventually be overcome. Many reconnaissance satellites today use passive

ESM systems of one type or another. These will be discussed in the next chapter.

The principal advantage of satellites as surveillance platforms is their ability to survey the entire globe, and their wide field of view. Even at low orbit, a satellite will be in radio range of vast areas of ocean, many hundreds of miles across and with probably hundreds of ship targets in view. However, this breadth of vision introduces its own problems of data analysis. The requirement is to identify each detection, so that it can be correlated with earlier detections of the same target obtained in earlier passes. If this is not done, the picture will be of limited operational value, since unless each detection can be sufficiently identified to distinguish it from the others in its area it will be impossible to correlate it with earlier detections of the same target in the previous pass—in other words target tracks cannot be developed. This enhances the value of passive ESM sensors which, as we have seen, have a good chance of being able to read a target's electronic signature. However, even with ESM sensors, there is so much data to analyse and correlate that it is beyond the capacity of a satellite's payload, however equipped. This has led to the current technique of telemetering the satellite's raw electronic data down to earth, where it can be processed, using the large computers available on land. This has the advantage that data from all satellites in orbit is brought together for correlation.

The technical and operational problems associated with satellite reconnaissance were difficult to overcome in the initial stages of the art. Now, however, with much higher loads being put into orbit, many of the earlier difficulties have been greatly reduced. As a result, regular and effective surveillance of ocean areas is a modern fact of life. Nevertheless, satellite reconnaissance techniques are very expensive; only the super powers operate fully developed systems, the output from which is made available to their allies. Naval commanders both gain and lose from the advent of such systems, since they are the recipients of friendly intelligence from their own sources, but at the same time exposed to the enemy's. The commander at sea will know when enemy satellites will pass over his area, and may reduce the risk of detection by closing down on radio and radar during the period they are in view. This, however, will severely inhibit his force's warning system and general combat readiness. The reconnaissance satellite exemplifies naval command and control in the electronic age. Satellites and computers have shrunk the world and fleets can no longer rely on hiding themselves at sea for extended periods. On the other hand, the force commander is now much more aware of what is happening in his area of operations.

3

The Electro-Magnetic Environment— Electronic Warfare

WE have seen how navies depend on their electronics for the majority of information reaching the command, and for control of ships, aircraft and weapons. Such dependence creates a potential weakness since it offers the opportunity to attack the electronic control systems rather than the weapons themselves. If an incoming missile splashes harmlessly into the sea, it is of relatively little concern to the defending ship whether it does so because it has been physically damaged by an anti-missile missile, or because its controls have been confused by an electronic jammer. The exploitation of the enemy's use of electronics, and the taking of measures to counter his use of such techniques, is known as Electronic Warfare, or EW.

In the early days of EW it was looked on as something of secret oddity in the context of defence equipment and tactics. In the Royal Navy, technical policy and equipment design was the responsibility of a group of highly qualified and enthusiastic experts, regarded as slightly eccentric. Development in the USN was on similar lines, and the cooperation established between the two navies during World War II was continued and extended. The stimuli of the sharing of ideas and competition in achievement benefited the evolution of new techniques and equipment in both navies. Nowadays EW has come of age and is no longer a hidden subject. In particular, it is no longer treated as a black art. Electronic Warfare is taken extremely seriously at all levels in modern navies and it is often said that the EW battle at the outset of an engagement will largely determine the overall outcome.

Much has been written on the subject, and there is a companion book in the present series devoted exclusively to it. In this chapter we consider EW in outline only, as seen from its relevance to command and control; its importance in this respect is obvious when one remembers that electronics provide the main source of information to the command and the only primary means of communication at sea.

The subject is wide and is divided into a number of related fields, as illustrated in Figure 3.1. Although the terminology may appear somewhat formidable, it is in fact quite logical. *Electronic Countermeasures*, or ECM, cover the use of techniques and equipment to counter or spoil the enemy's use of electronics;

FIGURE 3.1

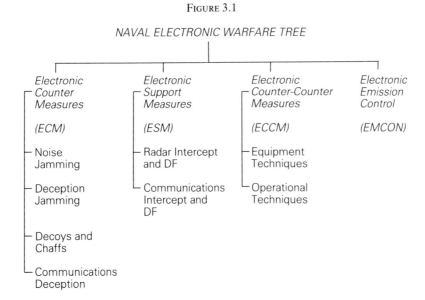

NAVAL ELECTRONIC WARFARE TREE

jamming is a well-known example. The second arm of EW is *Electronic Support Measures*, (ESM), which seek to exploit the enemy's use of electronics (rather than degrade them) to support one's own tactics. The interception and analysis of enemy transmissions is an example. The development of ECM and ESM has led to the antidote, namely *Electronic Counter-Countermeasures*, known as ECCM, the discipline which generates techniques designed to protect equipment against ECM and ESM. These are mostly technical in nature and built into the basic equipment as part of its design, but there are operational ECCM procedures as well. The final arm of EW shown in Figure 3.1 is sometimes considered to be part of ECCM, namely *Control of Electronic Emissions* or EMCON. This is however so important to command and control that in this book it is considered separately. It covers all measures taken to limit the use of electronics in one's own force in order to lessen one's own exposure to enemy ESM or ECM. We will now consider these four fields in greater detail.

ELECTRONIC COUNTERMEASURES

There is a large and varied array of ECM devices, but it will assist understanding to recognise two distinct operational objectives:

▶ To disrupt or confuse enemy surveillance and communications, so that he is unable to achieve what he intends from the use of his radar and communications.
▶ To reduce the lethality of the enemy's guns and missiles by spoiling the performance of the electronics on which such weapons rely for their effectiveness.

Some ECM equipments may be used in either role, but most equipment is specialised to one or the other.

Radar Noise Jamming

A transmission on the frequency of the target radar, modulated by noise, has the well-known effect of saturating the radar receiver and producing a continuous 'noisy' paint over the display. The effect is to mask weak echoes completely and to degrade the picture generally, so that even strong echoes may be missed. Strong noise jamming will fill the receiver through the aerial side lobes, which will cause the effect to show over the entire radar display screen; weaker jamming will, however, only affect the main lobe, and thus the azimuth sector embracing the jammer. Noise jamming can therefore disrupt radar surveillance and cause the enemy much confusion. However, there are considerable draw-backs attached to the use of this type of jamming, particularly by ships. It may alert an enemy aircraft to the presence of a ship, as it will pick up jamming, identifiable as a ship jammer, well outside radar detection range. While the jammer may successfully screen his own ship, it is much more difficult to screen others in the force, since to do this relies on entry via side lobes. Even if jamming is effective, it is relatively easy for the victim radar to reduce receiver gain, perhaps automatically, so that, while it lasts, jamming shows up as a spoke lying along the bearing of the jammer. Perhaps the greatest danger is that if noise jamming is used as a defence against incoming missiles, there is the possibility

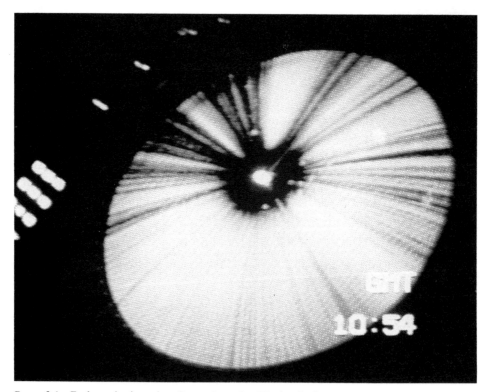

PLATE 3.1   Radar noise jamming. Strong jamming fills the display screen, rendering it useless for the detection of targets. (*Courtesy Racal Electronics*)

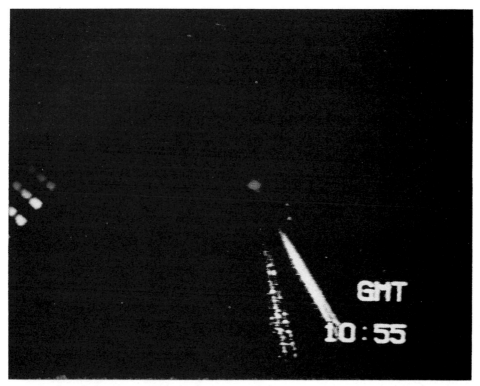

PLATE 3.2   Weaker jamming only affects the sector holding the jamming platform, thus revealing its bearing. It may be possible to detect radar echoes outside this sector.
(*Courtesy Racal Electronics*)

that the missile radar will automatically switch to the home-on-jam mode without the ship knowing it. The simple noise jammer is therefore a crude weapon and its use by ships is difficult and fraught with dangers as well as advantages. However, noise jammers are effective weapons for use by aircraft against ships, particularly in support of strikes. If employed at the moment when the raid is first detected, and especially if a number of aircraft jam from different directions, the confusion caused may well delay the true situation being appreciated in time for an effective response.

Communications Noise Jamming

Jamming an enemy communications circuit by transmitting on his frequency with a noise modulated signal will have the effect of disrupting reception, providing it is strong enough at the receiver. In practice this is difficult to achieve at long range, but relatively simple at short range. There are few attendant disadvantages such as those attached to anti-radar noise jamming; the main ones being that the jammer may interfere with one's own ship transmissions, and that the enemy circuit so jammed is not available for interception. In these days, however, most communications circuits are crypto-protected and yield little immediate information to the interceptor. Jamming at short range may be a useful method of disrupting and confusing an enemy's tactical communications and thus attacking his capacity to exercise command and control. It will be particularly effective if used at a critical moment, such as at the height of action or when first detected, and when combined with other forms of disruption, such as anti-radar jamming. Like radar jamming, communications jamming is best used as a weapon to support attack, and it is most likely to be used at sea by aircraft in support of strikes against forces of warships, to disrupt the coordination of force defence.

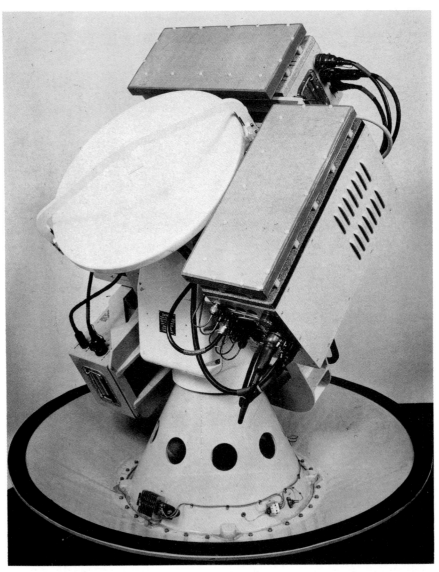

PLATE 3.3   The CYGNUS shipborne jammer, showing the narrow-beam dish aerial with other modules sited in close proximity. The whole arrangement is normally enclosed inside an electronically-translucent protective radome. (*Courtesy Racal Electronics*)

Deception Jamming

A more sophisticated type of radar jammer is provided by the false target generator, which aims to deceive a radar rather than disrupt it. This uses the ability to enter the receiver of a scanning radar through the side lobes, using pulses of the same size and shape as the radar itself produces through its main beam. Since the echo will appear on the radar display at the moment that the main lobe is looking in a different direction, it will appear to originate from that bearing, rather than from the direction of the jammer.

PLATE 3.4   Chaff used for decoying. The four echoes in a line, at the tip of the strobe marker, are caused by a frigate and three chaff clouds deployed by its rockets. A missile radar would probably be unable to distinguish which of these was the ship. (*Courtesy Chemring*)

Decoys and Chaff

Anti-ship missiles are a major threat to surface ships, and the development of counter-measures is an important naval priority. One method of defence is to place a physical object as a false target in the path of the incoming missile. The missile picks up the false target on its homing radar, perceives it to be a ship, selects it as the wanted target, locks-on and homes in. As the missile flies past the false target, it will, of course, lose it on its radar and will then revert to the radar search mode. However, if the false target has been correctly positioned relative to the ship, the missile will have passed by and the ship will be outside its search sector. The missile will therefore proceed harmlessly on its way. The processes are known as distraction and seduction. A variety of devices and materials can be used to provide such decoys.

Chaff is a material which has a variety of uses in EW; the most important naval application is for decoying enemy missiles, but it may be employed against navies in other ways. Chaff is the name given to small pieces of foil or conducting filament cut to a critical length (half the wavelength of the radar frequency) and used in quantity to cause radar reflection and thus induce radar echoes. Bundles of chaff, made up of millions of such dipoles are deployed by shell, rocket or missile, or deployed from aircraft, to create either area wide interference or

FIGURE 3.2   Seduction of missile by offboard decoy

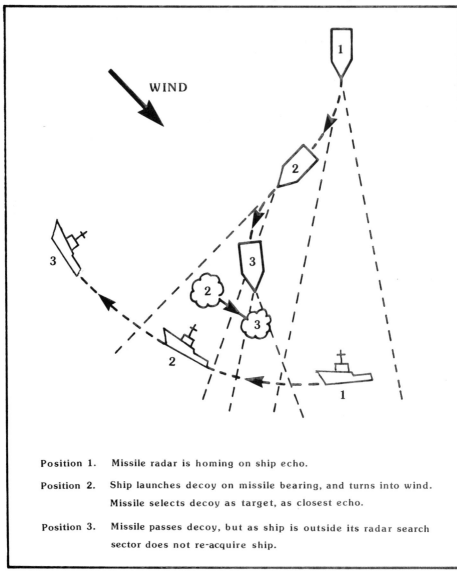

WIND

Position 1.   Missile radar is homing on ship echo.

Position 2.   Ship launches decoy on missile bearing, and turns into wind. Missile selects decoy as target, as closest echo.

Position 3.   Missile passes decoy, but as ship is outside its radar search sector does not re-acquire ship.

specific localised false echoes. Used by aircraft it can cause confusion, and perhaps mask other aircraft for a period like a smoke screen. This is an important use of chaff. However, chaff can also be used by navies to create false targets around ships in order to decoy incoming missiles, as described in the previous paragraph. Chaff is placed in position by rocket, usually in a pattern near the ship to ensure that the missile encounters the chaff as a target before the ship. The tactical procedures are complicated, as the rockets which dispense the chaff must be fired on the correct bearings at the correct time, and the ship then manoeuvred to maintain its position within the protective pattern as it drifts downwind. Moreover, during an extended battle, the pattern must be replaced, as the chaff clouds gradually disperse or fall into the sea. Future generations of missile radars may be able to distinguish between chaff and ship echoes, but chaff is currently a most effective method of self defence, and was much used by the Task Force during the Falklands Campaign against Exocet missiles.

Missiles may also be seduced from selecting their wanted targets by the use of decoys. The infra-red (IR) decoy is an important form of this device. Ships emit a

FIGURE 3.3.   Ship manoeuvring inside Chaff decoy pattern

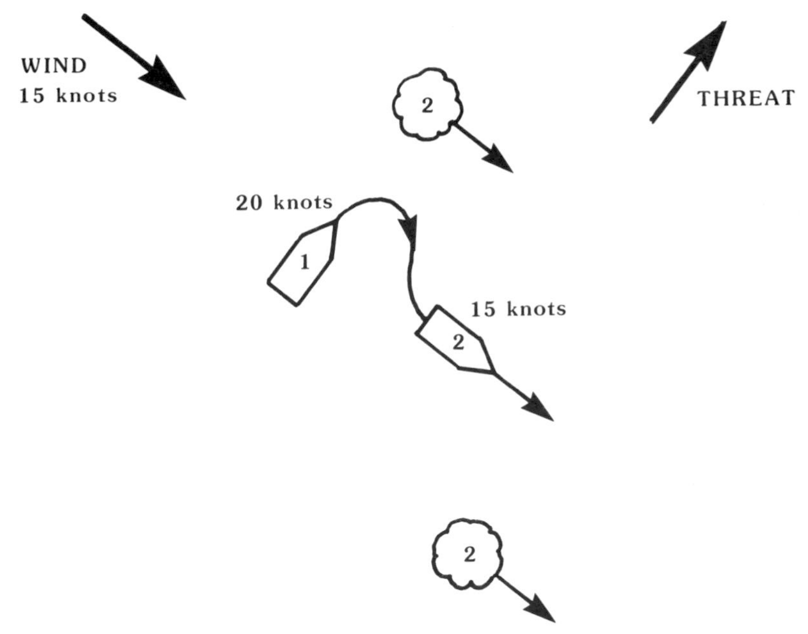

Position 1.	Ship detects threat and fires protective chaff pattern, immediately turning down wind and reducing speed.
Position 2.	Chaff clouds have formed. Ship has adjusted course and speed and moves down wind inside pattern.

lot of radiation in the infra-red region of the spectrum: examples are the hot funnel and exhaust plume and, at lower but detectable temperatures, ships' sides exposed to the sun. The resulting IR signature is a useful target for a missile to seek and many modern missiles use IR receivers as one method of terminal homing. IR decoys are usually flares deployed by rocket and suspended from parachutes. As with chaff, the main operational problem is to obtain enough warning to deploy them in time.

Communications Deception

Communications deception is achieved when false messages or information are received by an enemy who accepts them as real. It can be done either by transmitting false communications traffic on one's own circuits for an enemy to intercept thinking they are genuine, or by passing messages on an enemy circuit which appear to emanate from one of his units. The latter is known as spoofing. Communications deception can vary in scale from simple spoofing on a tactical net to large scale deception as part of a wider operational or strategic plan. The largest example of the latter is probably the Deception Plan used to support the Allied invasion of Normandy in 1944—Operation OVERLORD—where communications deception on a very large scale was used as part of a larger operation to convince the German High Command that the Normandy landings were a feint and that the real invasion would occur in the Pas de Calais. Deception on this scale is strategic in nature and requires vast resources. It is outside the scope of this book.

At a lower level, however, communications deception may be a theoretical option. Spoofing of tactical circuits is often referred to as if the technique was a practicable ploy. However, there are several serious difficulties and disadvantages. First, there is the fact that unless every detail is correct, the spoofer will almost immediately be identified as such. For example, on a tactical voice net, the accent, tone of voice and communications procedure must all fit—not an easy requirement to meet from an enemy unit. Second, many of the circuits on which spoofing would be most useful are nowadays protected by on-line cryptography or speech secrecy equipment, and cannot be entered by an enemy. Finally, a point which applies to all deception: deception that is recognised as such may do more harm than good. On the whole, communication deception is not as attractive operationally as it might appear and will rarely survive an initial success for more than a short time. Like so many other examples of active ECM it may therefore, if used at all, be best employed as a means of introducing temporary confusion at the height of an attack, when the enemy is attempting to direct his response and can ill afford any disturbance or confusion in his command and control.

ELECTRONIC SUPPORT MEASURES

The second branch of the EW tree encompasses what are now known as Electronic Support Measures, since the actions are undertaken in support of one's own operations, rather than to disrupt the enemy's operations which is the object of Electronic Countermeasures. These divisions were previously known as Active and Passive EW; active since ECM involves actions like transmitting to jam enemy transmissions or deploying decoys to confuse his control: passive EW because ESM relies on receiving (a passive activity) enemy transmissions. ESM is a most important arm of modern naval warfare, which fulfils three roles. First, it offers a primary method of warning and surveillance, independent of radar; second, it is a valuable adjunct to radar surveillance, as already explained in the previous chapter; third, it provides target identification, indication and control for ECM, which could not be used effectively without associated ESM.

ESM, since it relies on the enemy transmission and thus enemy cooperation, might be regarded as opportunistic and intrinsically unreliable. However, modern navies and air forces are so dependent on radar and communications for their fighting capability that the likelihood of intercepting enemy transmission is high. The inverse also applies. If the existence of ESM capabilities on one side forces the other to adopt general or partial radio and radar silence, a measure of tactical success is achieved very economically, since the enemy has been forced to weaken his fighting potential without a shot being fired. When considering the value of passive as opposed to active sensors, it is worth remembering that the two main human sensors, the eyes and the ears, are passive detectors. Indeed it is hard to quote many examples from nature of active sensors; the sonars of some birds and bats, and of whales and dolphins, spring most readily to mind. The nearest man can get to an active sensor is the use of an electric torch, or his motorcar headlights, but these are 'secondary systems' since the eyes receive reflected light transmitted from another source.

Passive interceptors have one other principal disadvantage over active systems—it is impossible to obtain the range of a detection accurately, although an estimate may be obtainable in some cases. Passive receivers if fitted with appropriate aerials and analysis equipment may yield the direction (usually known as the bearing) of a detection, and the technique is known as Direction Finding or DF. The bearing accuracy of DF varies widely, depending on the frequency and type of transmission, from ten degrees or more in the case of long distance DF of high frequency communications to a single degree or less in the case of anti-radar DF equipment. While a single bearing of an enemy trans-mission will certainly be of use operationally, an exact position is of far greater value, since it locates the platform accurately and enables a plot of its movement to be developed. To provide a position from ESM it is necessary to obtain two simultaneous bearings of the same detection from separated platforms, and then fix the position by triangulation. The accuracy of the resultant position is dependent on the accuracy of the bearings, the angle of cut and the accuracy with which the two platforms' positions are known and plotted. The process is also dependent on good communication between the two platforms.

Radar Intercept and DF

There are two important operational advantages obtainable from anti-radar ESM. First, ESM equipment has a range advantage over the target radar, which, providing the ESM aerial is sited high enough, will be detected at a greater range than that at which the radar will detect the ESM platform. The effect is similar to the well-known phenomenon of being able to see a car's headlights round a corner before the car itself is in sight; the scattering effect of the atmosphere enables the loom of the light to be seen first. Second, much information on the type of radar being intercepted can be deduced from signal analysis of the radar's characteristics such as radio frequency, pulse width, pulse repetition frequency and aerial rotation rate. These constitute the equivalent of a signature of the radar itself; furthermore, taken into conjunction with the signatures of other radars and emitters on the same bearing (and thus presumed to be onboard the same platform) they also lead to a deduction on the identity of the parent ship or aircraft. Apart from visual inspection, no information on the identity of a detected target is as complete or as reliable as that provided by ESM.

Sophisticated techniques have been developed for the rapid and accurate measurement of radar signal characteristics. Software based methods of comparing these characteristics with a library of known enemy and friendly emitter parameters enable the identity of target radars to be obtained very rapidly and then passed automatically into the command system to be correlated with radar and other tactical information. Such systems can also solve triangulation problems by automatic data exchange with other units, thus providing ESM-derived positions. Another feature of software-based ESM equipment is that a means of automatic warning can be provided; if the signature of a new detection agrees sufficiently with the parameters in a pre-set alarm device a warning can be triggered. Such automatic warning would, for example, be particularly valuable in the case of an incoming sea-skimmer missile, identified by ESM at extreme range before radar detection. It is also possible to make such a warning device initiate an automatic response, for example to launch decoys or fire an anti-missile missile. The use of such automatic weapons response is examined further in Chapter 6.

An important refinement of radar intercept techniques is available to aid a submarine on the surface or at periscope depth showing a snorkel, or a radar mast. In such an exposed situation, advanced warning of the approach of enemy search aircraft is of vital importance to the submarine captain; however, warning of the presence of an aircraft in the general area is of limited value by itself, since the submarine could be induced to dive unnecessarily if a passing aircraft was unlikely to approach close enough for detection. What is needed is warning of imminent detection. This information is provided by an ESM technique known as Reciprocal Intercept, whereby the echo signal strength available to the searching radar is deduced from the ESM intercept, and a broad measure obtained of the safety margin available to the submarine. This allows the submarine captain to continue with his operational task until it becomes essential to dive to avoid being detected.

The main ESM equipments in service today provide all-round-looking, wide band coverage, with high receiver sensitivity and near-instantaneous measurement of frequency and other parameters. Such systems are a notable improvement on the previous generation of ESM equipments. Since the new equipment has been introduced, naval officers have learnt to use it very effectively and attitudes have changed markedly towards ESM as a source of tactical informa-

PLATE 3.5   A typical modern ESM operator's console, showing the tote information on the VDU and the keyboard controls. The operator is wearing earphones and a boom microphone for internal communication with ship's officers. (*Courtesy Racal Electronics*)

tion. The new equipment—of which the Royal Navy's Outfits UAA1 is typical— are easy to operate, being fully digitalised and under keyboard control. They have extensive signal analysis and other user aids available on keyed call-up, including warning devices (as discussed in an earlier paragraph). The consoles from which they are operated are integral with any associated jammer controls, since ESM provides the surveillance and target indication needed for jammer operation.

Electronic Intelligence

In parallel with the rise in the importance of ESM there has been a marked increase in the scale and value of electronic intelligence (ELINT), that is the collection and use of intelligence derived from intercept of enemy electronic emissions. ELINT, together with its communications counterpart COMINT, form an important branch of Intelligence, known as signal intelligence (SIGINT). As the name implies, SIGINT provides intelligence from the interception and analysis of signals or emissions of all types; because of the differences in techniques and applications it is normally divided into communications and non-communications fields. As an intelligence activity, SIGINT is strategic in nature but, as we shall see, it has important operational and tactical applications. Since the latter use of ELINT and COMINT are analagous to ESM we are dealing with them in this book under that heading.

The term ELINT covers the collection and use of intelligence available from the interception of radars and similar electronic devices, principally in the frequency bands above those used for communications. The product of ELINT satisfies two main requirements. It provides operational intelligence, that is information of a general nature of immediate tactical or strategic interest, such as a deduction that the interception of a particular type of radar indicates the presence in that area of an enemy unit known to carry it. ELINT also provides the input to the long term data base of technical intelligence on enemy and friendly electronics. Such a data base has many uses, not the least of which is to serve tactical EW. Before an enemy radar can be jammed or DF'd it must be known to exist. Its operational function and what ships and aircraft carry it must also be known, together with its frequency and other characteristics, including its susceptibility to ECM. ELINT is collected by national specialist intelligence services but this information is supplemented by information obtained by operational units such as ships, submarines and aircraft in the course of operational deployment.

The fact that radar transmissions, and other emissions in the ELINT frequency bands, travel in straight lines limits the area over which they may be intercepted for ELINT purposes. The interceptor must be approximately within radio horizon range, a matter of 15–20 miles in the case of ships and, say, 100–250 miles in the case of aircraft, depending on height. An important exception occurs in the case of satellites, which can be considered as aircraft at extreme height for the purpose of ELINT interception. Since a satellite is in view of the whole of the earth's surface beneath it, any radar (indeed any emission) within the satellite footprint—the term used to describe the oval area on the earth's surface within its coverage—can be intercepted, subject to the receiver being tuned to cover its frequency, and the aerial pointing in its direction; this makes the ESM satellite a most important method of collecting ELINT. In many ways a satellite is an ideal platform for a passive wideband radar intercept receiver, which may be within reach of hundreds of transmissions of interest at any time. Intercepts are received raw and passed via the down link to earth, where they are analysed by computer and the intelligence disseminated for operational and strategic use. A variety of satellite orbits may be used, the choice depending on which part of the earth is to be covered and the degree of discrimination required. The lower the orbit the narrower the swathe of territory covered, and the more rapid the angular velocity of travel. It is expensive in satellite resources to provide continuous coverage of a particular area; regular coverage by patterned transits is the more normal mode.

Communications Intelligence

Radio communications transmissions are also prone to interception and, like radar, they yield intelligence, although of a different type. First, they may be DF'd, thus exposing the position of the transmitting ship or aircraft. The information derived from this technique is not important in the case of short range communications, for example UHF circuits used in a task force, since, if communication is taking place, the presence of the target platform is probably known already to the interceptor. However, with long range communication, particularly High Frequency (HF) circuits used for world wide ship-to-shore communication, the effect is dramatic. Shore based DF stations, linked by high speed data circuits, can triangulate an HF transmission virtually anywhere in the world. Although the accuracy is not high (typically of the order of 10–100 miles) the fact that a ship or submarine is in the approximate area can be of great operational consequence. The vulnerability to DF means that in wartime the use of HF as a means of ship to shore communication is heavily constrained. For many operations, radio silence in this and other long range frequency bands is normal until the presence of the unit is reckoned to be known to the enemy. Satellite communications, which we shall see in a later chapter are the modern substitute for HF, do not suffer the same restriction as they cannot be DF'd in the same way.

The other type of information available from the interception of communications is the intelligence available from analysis of the traffic. This can be considered at two levels. The first is the information available from study of traffic patterns, such as the fact that a new circuit has been opened or that there is a marked increase in traffic levels. Deductions about units involved may also be derived from analysis of callsigns. Of greater operational significance is the intelligence available from analysis of texts, if available. This may be of a strategic or tactical nature, depending on the circuit being intercepted. However the introduction of high-grade on-line cryptographic and speech secrecy equipment has meant that most vital circuits these days are protected from crypto-analysis and even where on-line systems are not used, high grade off-line cryptography will give similar protection.

ELECTRONIC COUNTER-COUNTER MEASURES

From the historical beginnings of such activity, the evident dangers attached to an enemy's use of ECM and ESM have ensured that protective techniques have been developed in parallel—now known collectively as Electronic Counter-Counter Measures or ECCM. Like ECM and ESM, ECCM are divided into different categories, the most important division being between those which are designed and built into equipment, and those which depend on its method of operation.

The best means of ensuring that neither ECM or ESM can be practised against you is to arrange that the enemy is either unaware that your equipment is radiating, or if he is, that he cannot receive its transmissions for long enough to deploy jammers, intercept receivers or a DF chain against it. This approach has led to a variety of 'frequency agile' techniques, from the simple operational ploy of changing frequency as often as practicable, to sophisticated automatic frequency agile equipment. Here even the dwell time on each pulse may be significant, since the longer an enemy is given to analyse a possible pulse the more likely it will be recognised as a target. Frequency agility is a most important anti-jamming and anti-intercept technique; when used to protect communications circuits it is usually referred to as 'frequency hopping'.

A different approach is to arrange that transmissions are concealed in the radio background noise so that, although they are radiated on a nominally constant frequency, they cannot be recognised as significant, even if intercepted. The most effective method uses what is known as spread spectrum techniques. The signal is transmitted as a series of formatted pulses, the coding of which conveys the information to be communicated. The coding pattern is randomised using a cryptographically generated key, so that it is meaningless to the enemy interceptor. At the friendly receiver the inverse of the same cryptographic key is used to recognise the transmitted pulse stream amongst the noise and thus to recover the wanted information. Spread spectrum has been made possible by the introduction of digital techniques, and it is a powerful electronic tool, which may be used in conjunction with other ECCM techniques such as frequency agility to give extra security.

ECCM is a wide subject and space does not permit us to examine the many other techniques in use. The advent of ECCM has spawned a jargon of its own: ECM resistance or ECM resistant circuits, low probability of intercept (LPI) and anti-jamming capability (AJ) are examples of terms which are applied to the equipment they protect rather than the specific technique in use. Indeed it is not always clear where ECCM ends and normal equipment design begins.

Emission Control (EMCON)

From the point of view of command and control perhaps the most important ECCM measure to consider is the policy for the control of electronic emissions, namely the extent to which radio and radar equipment should be permitted to be used. In years gone by, EMCON was a relatively simple matter and concerned the question of whether radio silence should be broken. It was normal to maintain silence on leaving harbour to avoid being DF'd, and opening up as soon as the position of the force has been discovered by the enemy. Perhaps the most dramatic example of this tactic was the use of radio silence by the Japanese fleet during its approach to the attack on Pearl Harbor in 1941. The force sailed undetected from Japan to within 200 miles of Hawaii, an important contribution to the achievement of surprise.

Nowadays the problem is less simple; electronics have become more complex and diverse, and vital to warning and fighting capability. It is therefore far more difficult to strike the right balance between restricting and allowing emissions. The EMCON policy must also embrace the use of sonar and underwater emissions which can also be detected over long range; this subject will be addressed in the next chapter. The sort of questions that must be posed and answered by the commander and his staff before and during an operation include:

Is it worthwhile silencing some radars and HF communications, and accepting the resulting operational penalty, whilst permitting the use of other electronic equipment?

Can the force afford not to use active sonar in order to prevent long range underwater detection?

Even if we do, will our ship-generated noise not reveal the force to enemy submarines?

How soon will the location of the force be discovered by enemy reconnaissance aircraft using radar, or satellite and other types of long range surveillance, regardless of whether electronic emissions are allowed or not?

Will the commander know when this happens?

The commander of a modern task force may come to the conclusion that the likelihood of detection is so high that he cannot afford to reduce the fighting capability provided by radar and sonar surveillance, weapon control, aircraft direction and radio communications, and must allow unrestricted emission. In other situations he may decide to apply strict silence for a limited period to conceal the fact that the force has put to sea and to relax this later. In the case of single vessel operations, it may be sensible to adopt a highly restrictive EMCON policy. For submarines, it will usually be essential. Whatever the circumstances, the choice of the EMCON policy in force, and its continual review and adjustment is one of the main concerns of the command.

EW and Command and Control

Electronic Warfare is a large subject, and to place it in context we must attempt to summarise its effects on naval command and control. In some ways it would appear to be even-handed in its effects: jammers, decoys, ELINT, DF etc. can be used by either side. This, however, is an over simplification. On the whole, EW creates more problems than it solves for command and control, which is nowadays completely dependent on radio and radar and other emitting devices. ECM and ESM exploit this dependence and thus threaten and complicate the command and control task. Account should be taken of the fact that decoys and other ECM devices reduce the lethality of missiles, and that ESM can give excellent warning and identification. Nevertheless many naval commanders would consider themselves better able to direct operations and control a modern sea battle if electronic warfare did not exist.

4

Sonar and the Underwater Environment

NAVIES and their supporting aircraft must move and fight in two contrasting arenas. The first is above the sea, which, as we have seen in the last two chapters, is dominated by the use of electronics for communications, surveillance and the control of weapons. From the point of view of tactics and command, this is a relatively simple environment. The behaviour of radio waves is on the whole predictable, and information travels at the speed of light with little distortion; as a result the picture available from surveillance is on the whole good, and reports and instructions can be passed accurately and rapidly. The other world in which navies must move and fight is underwater, a totally different story. This chapter examines the underwater environment and how command and control is exercised in it.

To detect an object from another point, or to communicate between two points, it is necessary for energy to pass between them. The only form of energy that propagates effectively underwater is sound. There is little prospect of the development of 'underwater radar' based on electro-magnetic waves because water, being an electrical conductor, will not support radio propagation over tactically significant distances. Sonar is the acoustic equivalent of radar, and although more variable, is the only prime method available for detection and communication underwater. Methods such as magnetic anomaly detection (MAD), infra-red detection of wakes and surface scars, and the use of lasers do not at present offer sufficiently effective performance to be considered as more than secondary systems. The properties of sound in sea water dictate why this is so, and to understand sonar and its limitations it is necessary to examine these in some detail.

The Behaviour of Sound in Sea Water

One of the distinguishing characteristics of sound in sea water is its relatively low speed of propagation, on average about 5000 feet or 1500 metres per second. This compares with the speed of light, 186,000 miles per second, at which radar propagates. Information obtainable by sonar is therefore inevitably stale compared with radar. Although the effect is normally unimportant at close range it may become a major limitation at longer range.

Another important feature of the propagation of sound in water is the physical limit to the intensity that the medium can support. If attempts are made to generate sound at energy levels above this, the resulting pressure wave will produce negative peaks that are at or below the pressure at which water vaporises. This produces small pockets of near vacuum and the process of wave propagation breaks down, the energy being lost instead to heat and acoustic noise. The effect is known as cavitation and it will occur if an active sonar is overdriven; it will also occur at the tips of propeller blades driven at high speeds. Cavitation produces bubbles which collapse as the water fills the vacuum again, and this produces low level sound of a noiselike character which of course radiates and is detectable. Susceptibility to cavitation decreases as depth, and thus ambient pressure, increases. The existence of cavitation means that active sonars, which must transmit high energy levels, have to be designed with large underwater arrays. Another effect is to render ships using high speed even more noisy and thus detectable than would otherwise be the case.

Perhaps the most important characteristic of sound in water is the way in which the energy is propagated, and becomes attenuated. Several factors make sonar transmissions difficult to predict. To begin with sound does not travel in straight lines, since the wave front or beam is bent by the refractive effect of variations in temperature, pressure and salinity present in sea water, the dominant factor

FIGURE 4.1   Refraction of sound in sea water

Showing effects of changes in Temperature and Pressure

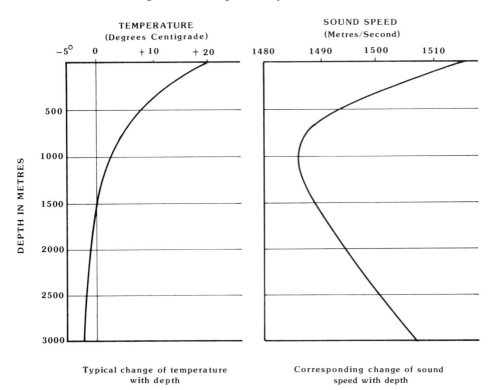

being temperature. The behaviour of sound waves and sonar beams is particularly affected by temperature gradient, that is the variation of temperature with depth, and certain conditions create layers which reflect or duct sonar signals, and may inhibit surveillance. The local patterns of temperature gradient vary from ocean to ocean, with the time of year, and with weather. Sonar conditions, and thus sonar performance, can therefore vary widely.

The effect of temperature gradient and the existence of layers and ducts is so fundamental to the use of sonar and the conduct of underwater warfare that steps must be taken during naval operations to discover the local conditions. The gradient is measured using sensors which are deployed over the ship's side to record sound speed against depth, from which the temperature gradient and thus the local pattern of sonar layers and ducts can be deduced. This is often referred to as 'taking a dip'. Knowledge of such local patterns obviously enables ships and commanders to be aware of the sonar conditions in which they must operate, and the sort of detection ranges they can expect; in addition it allows them to deploy sonars at optimum depth, and enables submarine commanders to use layers in order to remain concealed in what are known as shadow zones.

Another factor affecting sonar coverage is the reflection, scattering and absorption caused by the sea bottom and sea surface. Both boundaries will cause reflection of sound, although the degree varies with the conditions: both also cause scattering, the sea bottom, in particular, if it is rocky. A mud bottom will cause some absorption. The combined effects of these phenomena are complex but relatively predictable and can result in sound being trapped and propagating over greater distances than if such boundaries did not exist. They may also assist sonar coverage by filling in shadow zones.

FIGURE 4.2   Underwater Acoustic Ray Paths

(1000 metre depth of water, with reflecting bottom)

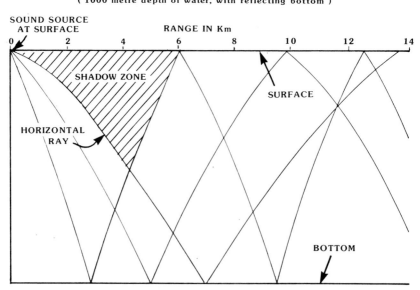

Typical acoustic ray paths with sound/speed profile as shown in Figure 4.1

Finally we must note the noise and path loss associated with the use of the sea as a propagating medium. Sea water absorbs energy in the form of heat loss as the sound wave propagates, which causes attenuation or path loss; the effect increases with frequency. Back scattering occurs as the sound wave interacts with innumerable minute marine organisms and this causes the noise known as reverberation; this is an important inhibition on effective sonar range. Reverberation is usually worse in shallow water and, in this case, is caused by back scattering due to the roughness of the surface and bottom boundaries. The sea is also a source of environmental noise, rather like the static found in the radio spectrum. This is caused by a variety of factors, such as the acoustic disturbance of surface waves, tidal flows and wave motion over rocks, and man-made noise such as the propeller and hull noises caused by shipping. The combined effect is to reduce the signal-to-noise ratio of wanted sound.

Classification

There is a further related difficulty in the use of sonar, namely the identification of the nature of detections. A solid object such as a submarine will cause the sound beam to reflect in similar fashion to the reflection of radar waves by metal objects like ships. However, other solid objects, such as whales, shoals of smaller fish and wrecks will also cause sonar echoes, known as 'non-sub'. Moreover non-solid phenomena like the wakes of ships or submarines, or knuckles of water caused by the rudders of ships turning at speed will also create sufficient disturbance of the sound wave to cause some of the energy to return as an echo. The extent to which sonar will provide ambiguous detections is much greater than similar problems with radar, where the main difficulty is to distinguish hostile from friendly. Classification of a sonar contact as 'sub' or 'non-sub' is the first vital step in using a detection to hunt an enemy submarine. As we shall see later, the use of passive sonar can greatly speed this process since direct interception of the sound generated by submarines, fish and the like (instead of an artificially induced echo) can yield positive and immediate information on the source.

The preceding sections of this chapter are a highly condensed version of a subject on which whole books have been written, but they illustrate the main technical features of the underwater world. It is an extremely difficult environment for navies, in which sonar, the only primary method of detection, is limited in range, unreliable in coverage, and greatly affected by the tactical behaviour of both the sonar platform and its target. The submarine, which has introduced underwater warfare, tends to benefit most from this situation, relying on stealth and the ability to remain undetected. The resulting inability to provide radar-equivalent surveillance of the tactical area in which the submarine operates is a grave disadvantage to the defensive anti-submarine forces located on and above the sea surface. We shall be returning in more detail to this theme later.

Sonar—General Characteristics

Seamen have been aware for many generations that sound travels underwater; noises of the sea can be heard in quiet conditions below decks in any vessel lying at anchor. German submarines used sound sensing devices known as hydrophones in World War I to detect shipping. The Allies also used hydrophones to locate and hunt submarines from anti-submarine escorts. These devices were passive, that is they sensed the sound emitted by the target. It is relatively easy for a submarine to make a significant reduction in the noise it emits by going slow and reducing machinery speeds, although this will inhibit its tactical freedom. A more positive means of detecting submarines was obviously a tactical requirement. After the war, the British Admiralty set up the famous ASDIC Committee to investigate how to combat the submarine menace. Their recommendations led to the development in the 1920s and 1930s of active equipment, which bore the name ASDIC until superseded by the American term 'sonar' in World War II. ASDIC operated on the principle later adopted by radar, namely, that sound should be beamed towards the target, producing an echo which could be sensed using the same equipment in reverse mode. Sonars operate as active or passive equipments and many are designed to cover both modes and allow a choice to be made as tactics require. We shall be looking at the characteristics of each mode of operation in more detail below.

The coverage provided by sonar is far more restricted than radar. Although sound can travel long distances, particularly if trapped within layers and ducts, it is difficult to rely on such modes of propagation for warning of submarine approach. The submarine captain will be aware of the existing thermoclinal conditions and can optimise his tactics to avoid detection. Moreover, the anti-submarine defence may not have a suitable sonar or platform to deploy at the correct depth to exploit such conditions. In particular, since the defence will not know where the submarine is and what approach he will take, sonar coverage cannot be optimised against him. This example illustrates several general points which distinguish underwater surveillance from the above water equivalent. Radar, if of suitable type and power, will illuminate an extensive and complete volume of air around its platform and any reflective object within that volume will be detected. Sonar cannot provide the same facility. Its coverage will be patchy, since the thermocline layering will inhibit sound reaching or coming from areas quite close. In addition, unlike radar, sonar may require a number of specialist equipments to optimise coverage. Finally, as already noted, the coverage provided by sonar is dependent on the behaviour of both platform and target—the platform must be at correct depth and cannot move at speeds which make it too noisy to receive sound signals; and the target can (albeit at possible tactical disadvantage) choose optimum depth and speed to avoid detection. Neither of these inhibitions affect radar to the same degree, which is largely unaffected by platform and target behaviour.

To obtain a detection, sound must pass from the target to the sonar platform. In the case of active sonar it must of course first pass out from the platform to the target, where it is partially reflected to cause a return echo. There are two modes in which this process can occur. The normal mode is the direct path, which will usually not be straight, but bent by the various ducts and layers encountered. However, the process is fairly straightforward, and, in good conditions, will provide detection ranges of several thousands of metres in the case of active sonar and perhaps tens of thousands of metres for passive sonar against a noisy target. This range advantage of about 5:1 is one of the advantages of using the passive mode. Note, however, the qualifying phrase 'in good conditions'. In many states of the weather and time of year, and with marked differences in the oceanography of different sea areas, the figures quoted must be viewed as maximum operational range, which will more often than not be reduced by layering and the other impediments to the passage of sound in sea water discussed above.

Another method of obtaining sonar coverage is to make use of convergence zones. In the previous paragraph we considered sonar beams which were broadly horizontal in nature and which, apart from the effects of ducting, travelled in nominally straight lines. In practice, sound which is directed downwards is gradually bent upwards by the refractive effect of the increase of pressure with depth. Thus, provided the water is deep enough, an active sonar beam will be returned to the surface at a point known as the 'first convergence zone'. Here it will be reflected by the surface to repeat the process to the 'second convergence

FIGURE 4.3   Convergence Zone Propagation

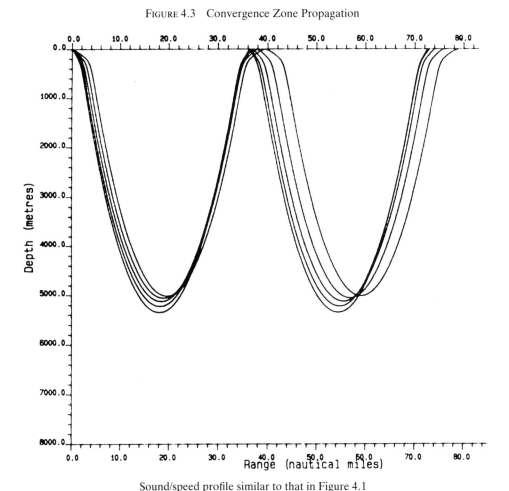

Sound/speed profile similar to that in Figure 4.1

zone', although there will be considerably less energy in this second leg, due to absorption loss. The process can be used in the active or passive mode, but requires both high transmitter power and high receiver sensitivity. Because propagation occurs mainly below the relatively shallow depths at which thermoclinal layering can occur, it is far more consistent than the normal mode discussed above. However, it is available only when the right conditions exist. The first convergence zone occurs at a distance from the sonar of about 30 miles in the North Atlantic and 20 miles in the Mediterranean, subsequent zones repeating the same interval. The width of the zone is typically of the order of 10 per cent of its range. This method, although requiring high power and large sonar arrays, does offer a fairly reliable method of long-range sonar surveillance, and is much used by the United States Navy.

Types of Sonar

Sonars can be divided into various categories. The first distinguishes them by the type of platform. Hull-mounted sonars are self-evident, being fixed installations fitted in ships and submarines and housed in bubble-like protrusions to the hull near the bows known as 'domes'. These are flooded with sea water, to put the transducer in acoustic contact with the medium but isolated from external water flow. The shell of the dome is transparent to sound, thus allowing it to leave and enter without loss or distortion, but strong enough to protect it from damage from collision with fish or debris.

Two types of sonar are towed astern. *Towed arrays* are highly sensitive equipments, the transducing arrays of which are trailed behind the ship or submarine in long cylinders or flexible objects like thick ropes. *Variable depth sonars* (VDS) are sonars installed in small torpedo-like hulls which are towed behind ships, and some helicopters, at a set depth. A *dunking sonar* is an equipment of cylindrical shape which is deployed vertically from a helicopter when stationary in the hover. *Bottom mounted sonars* are equipments implanted on the sea bed; information is passed ashore by cable. A further type is the *torpedo mounted sonar*, rather like the radar homers in missiles, which uses sound to guide the torpedo to its target.

Sonars may also be deployed by free floating devices known as **sonobuoys**. These enable aircraft to obtain sonar information. The aircraft lays a number of buoys in a pattern and the sonar information from those in contact with the submarine are passed by radio to the aircraft. When correlated, this gives an approximate position and movement of the submarine; the aircraft can then extend the pattern so as to maintain contact. Sonobuoys are a most valuable method of harnessing the mobility of aircraft for anti-submarine warfare. They may also be used by helicopters.

The other main categorisation of sonars divides them, as we have seen, into active and passive equipments. As this determines their principal operating characteristics we shall examine each type in some detail.

PLATE 4.1   Dome being fitted to the bow sonar array of a diesel-electric submarine. (*Courtesy Plessey*)

Active Sonar

An active sonar set is, in its essentials, the underwater equivalent of a radar. Its advantage over passive sonar is that it provides a positive method of search, which does not rely on the target behaving in a manner that will expose it to detection. Sound is introduced into the sea by means of a transducer, which can be likened to a loudspeaker intended to work in water. The most common type uses a phenomenon known as the piezo-electric effect. Some crystals, such as quartz, change their shape under the influence of an electro-static field, and conversely generate small electric voltages under the influence of pressure. Practical transducers use a number of pieces of piezo-electric material connected to a metal diaphragm in contact with the water. This is made to oscillate at the required frequency by applying high alternating voltage, which causes energy to be projected into the water as a sound wave at the same frequency. The sound thus created is concentrated into a beam by mounting several transducers in an appropriately shaped array, and is generated at high levels of energy for short bursts, known as pulses. Each pulse travels out along its beam until it encounters a solid object which causes it to be partially reflected. This reflected energy, which is, of course, an echo, spreads out from the object and some of it returns to impinge on the transducer diaphragm, causing the inverse of the transmission sequence. The pressure on the diaphragm causes electrical voltages at the sound frequency, which is then amplified and presented in the earphones of the sonar operator as the well known 'ping' of a received sonar echo. Modern equipment automates this process, so the returned echo can be recognised electronically and processed with other information in tactical computer systems. During the time that the transmission to and from the target has occurred the transducer has remained on the same bearing, otherwise it would not pick up the returning echo, which must be 'in the beam' to be audible. The direction of the transducer therefore indicates the direction of the object causing the echo. The range of the object is given by the time interval, as with radar.

The basic sonar described above, which produces a single beam and is therefore sometimes known as a 'searchlight sonar', is used to sweep arcs of coverage from the transmitting platform. The maximum likely range of detection is a crucial factor. As we have seen, no set figure for this is possible, since it varies with the current sonar conditions as well as the characteristics of the equipment. The sea state, the ocean in which operations are occurring, and the time of year are but some of the things which influence effective sonar range for a given type of sonar. However, to give a comprehensible picture, some generalisation is necessary. We can therefore reckon that, in good conditions, which could be taken as winter in the North Atlantic in fair weather and moderate sea state, the extreme range for modern active sonars could be, say, 6000 metres or more. Poor conditions would reduce this to 2000 metres or less. The estimated figure for sonar operating range is assessed at regular intervals and kept set on the equipment. A sonar using one rotating beam must remain on the same bearing until the pulse has gone out to extreme range, found its target, and returned; the transducer is then trained to the new bearing and a further pulse transmitted. The slowness of this procedure, stemming from the speed of sound in water, means that most searchlight sonars are used to cover arcs or sectors rather than provide all-round coverage.

Considerable improvement on the above performance may be obtained when using sophisticated modern sonars, with high power and all-round multiple fixed beam coverage, employing complex swept frequency techniques. These are known as panoramic sonars and such equipments are normally fitted in sub-marines and ASW vessels nowadays.

Active sonar is used less today than in the past but, despite its limitations, it remains a vital component of the ASW armoury, having a number of pros and cons. Range is considerably less than that usually obtained by passive means and classification is often difficult. In addition, an active sonar will act as a beacon, being easily detectable and recognisable by enemy passive equipments up to tens of miles away; this characteristic virtually denies its use by submarines in most situations and makes its use by surface ships operationally unattractive. On the other hand, active sonar gives a direct measure of target range, which is not available from passive sonar and, being active, is a positive method which does not rely on the target emitting the required degree of noise. Active sonar does provide a valuable bonus not provided by passive equipments, nor for that matter normally available from radar. The low speed of sound in water means that the target's relative speed of approach or withdrawal will show as a change of frequency in the returned echo, arising from the doppler effect. This means that active sonar detection will normally yield a good indication of target rate of approach as well as its position. Doppler can also be put to good use in other ways, for example to reduce the effect of reverberations. For all these reasons active sonar has tended to become the mode used to enable submarines, detected by other means, to be attacked, rather than providing the anti-submarine screens of the past.

Passive Sonar

The development of towed arrays, coupled with the operational disadvantages of active sonar, has led to a reappraisal of the relative value of passive sonar to surface ships in recent years. It has always been regarded as the prime mode in submarines. Passive sonar in its simplest form is an active sonar used in the passive mode, that is with only its receive components in operation. The active components can be brought into use when required. Many modern sonars, however, are designed for passive use only. Although only a bearing of the target can be obtained, some indication of range can be deduced from the intensity of the received signal. There are several important advantages in using passive sonar for surveillance. One is the generally greater range of detection against noisy targets compared with active sonar. As with radar and radio emissions, it is difficult for ships and submarines to avoid creating detectable noise. Machinery clanks or hums, ships moving through the water make wake and wash noise, and propellers emit noise with identifiable signatures and beat. Measures to identify and reduce ship noise have become an important technical subject; suppression not only protects the vessel but, by lowering the background noise, increases the effectiveness of its own sonar. As high-powered sonar is probably the most detectable and dangerous of all ship noises, another advantage of using passive sonar is the simple fact that active sonar is not used at the same time. Another operationally useful feature is that target information is available continuously, unlike the repetitive 'pinging' involved with active sonar.

An important advantage of passive sonar is that detections are easier to classify. Non-sub noises such as those emanating from fish, or swirls of water, which cause such problems to active sonar, are immediately identifiable and may not even get as far as becoming reported detections. Stationary objects, like wrecks and rocks, do not emit sound and are not detected at all. Sounds coming from ships underway will often have characteristics like the beat of propellers and machinery noises, which will provide a considerable degree of identification. Submarines intending to remain hidden will be quiet targets and, if detected at all, will probably be recognisable as such. As with radar, in modern sonars the recognition of such noise patterns has nowadays been automated. As a result, it is often possible to provide target identification at the same time as detection.

In submarines, the performance of modern panoramic passive sonars is such that many submarine captains consider that they have a better tactical picture of their environment than their adversaries on the surface. This is probably due in large measure to the fact that the submarine, running quiet and at optimum depth is an ideal sonar platform. In surface ships and aircraft the use of passive sonar can, broadly speaking, be divided into two main fields. First its use in the local tactical area, where it takes the place of active sonar in providing local surveillance and warning of the approach of submarines that threaten the force; and second its use as a longer range surveillance sensor where it provides an important contribution to general ocean surveillance systems. The next section of this chapter will look at the use of sonar for anti-submarine surveillance in the vicinity of a task force, where passive techniques will provide the main coverage, backed by the use of active sonar for the prosecution of contacts. Similar procedures apply to sonar used to protect convoys.

Use of Sonar in a Naval Task Force

In the vicinity of the force there will be a variety of sonars in use in different platforms. Ships such as AS frigates will deploy either hull-mounted equipment (in many cases active/passive sonars) or, if so fitted, variable depth sonars. Hull-mounted equipment can be of a very modern design and capability such as the Royal Navy 2016, manufactured by Plessey. This is an all-round-looking sonar

PLATE 4.2   Sonar Operators' console. (*Courtesy Plessey*)

with impressive control and analysis facilities housed in an operator's console which can be connected to the ship's tactical computer system. Such a set while in the active mode for tracking and engagement of submarine contacts, can also be used passively to detect torpedoes. Older vessels will have older equipment and these will probably be sector scanning, and with simpler controls.

Variable depth sets (VDS) are now fitted in many ASW vessels. Such a set is housed in a towed body, which is normally stowed onboard in a gantry cradle, and streamed astern when required; its hydrodynamic shape and control surfaces then pull it down to operating depth, which will be determined by the ship's speed. The towing cable also carries electrical power down to the towed body, and the received sonar signal up to the ship. The advantage of VDS is that it may be possible to stream the towed body below any shallow duct if present. In addition, the sonar is deployed clear of the ship's own noise. The penalty associated with VDS is the size and weight of its handling gear, which indirectly imposes an important constraint on performance; there is a practical upper limit on the length of cable which can be carried, since the more cable the larger and heavier its stowage drum and winch.

Whatever sonar equipment is carried, most anti-submarine vessels will be deployed relatively close to the main body or convoy, or whatever force is being protected against submarine attack, to provide the inner ring of surveillance or

FIGURE 4.4   Variable Depth Sonar System

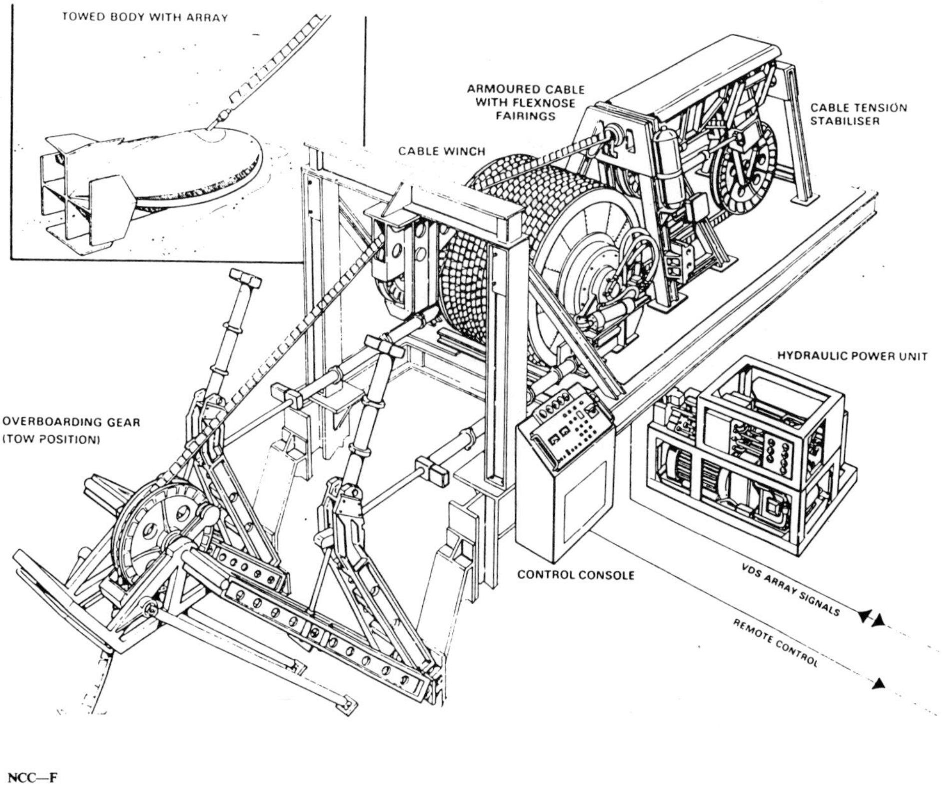

A VDS system, showing towed body, winch, and handling and deployment gear

anti-submarine screen. This will place them in positions from which attacking submarines are likely to be detectable, and in awkward and obstructive locations for submarines manoeuvring to attack; it will also enable them to launch immediate counter-attacks against incoming submarines. Nowadays, this ring or screen of AS vessels will probably be supplemented by helicopters, one of the most important modern additions to the anti-submarine armoury. All RN

PLATE 4.3   Sea King helicopter recovering its sonar from the dip. (*Courtesy Westland Helicopters*)

frigates carry AS-equipped helicopters, as do carriers and other large warships. The principal advantages of AS helicopters are their mobility and versatility. They can be used to plug gaps in the screens formed by AS vessels, or stationed further out on the bows of the force; they can then be moved quickly to new positions when required. Their dunking sonar can be lowered to optimum operating depth, thus perhaps providing more effective sonar cover than depth-limited ships' equipment. Large helicopters can carry AS weapons as well as sonar, and will be in an ideal position to carry out urgent attacks on submarine contacts. Many submarine captains consider helicopters their biggest threat when approaching a force to attack.

Still further out from the force will be the areas patrolled by cooperating fixed wing maritime aircraft, either carrier-borne or shore based. As well as using radar to detect snorkelling submarines, they will put down extended barriers of sonobuoys, carefully positioned to cover likely areas of submarine transit. Like the AS helicopter these aircraft will carry AS weapons, probably anti-submarine homing torpedoes, and once a confirmed enemy contact is detected and its position narrowed sufficiently, they will attack it. Some fixed wing aircraft still carry the magnetically activated sensor known as Magnetic Anomaly Detection equipment (MAD). This utilises the magnetic effect of the steel structure of a submarine hull. The aircraft flies low along a path judged from sonar detections to take it over or near the submarine. If it succeeds in passing within a few hundred metres of the submarine the MAD equipment will detect perturbations in the earth's magnetic field caused by the presence of the submarine, and will register a contact. MAD, however, requires the submarine to be at shallow depth to register any reaction, and even then covers only a relatively small circle of detection. Moreover, because of its short range, MAD cannot be used for surveillance or search, only for localising a contact already detected by sonar. It has particular operational value for use in shallow seas and coastal waters, where the submarine cannot operate at great depth.

Passive sonar coverage may also be provided in the outer tactical areas by ships equipped with what are known as towed arrays. These are highly sensitive equipments, capable of detecting low intensity sound at long range, which exploit the various modes in which sonar propagates. There are a variety of types of towed array, but their main characteristics are common to all. Sensitivity is obtained by the length of the array and the large number of transducers; these are individually connected to a computer via the towing cable, which also carries electrical current to the array. The sound pattern in each transducer is analysed and correlated with that in the others, and the differences in times of arrival of detected contacts measured to yield bearing. Maximum sensitivity is obtained by 'broadside fire', as the array detects targets best when they are at right angles to its axis; this means that the ship must direct its course to optimise surveillance and resolve any ambiguities. Careful choice of changes in course may also enable the vessel to obtain an indication of range by target motion analysis. Speed must be chosen carefully to avoid making ship noise and to ensure that the array streams correctly. In some circumstances, the towing vessel may use a 'sprint and drift' mode of advance, in which it executes a burst of speed to make ground in the required direction, followed by a period of quiet slow-speed operation whilst surveillance is carried out. The necessity to manoeuvre to optimise use of the array, coupled with the fact that to exploit the equipment to the full it should be clear of the force with its noise, means that towed array ships are usually stationed well out. They act as sonar pickets, perhaps several tens of miles ahead and on the wings of the general advance. Such extended disposition is compatible not only with the optimum use of towed array equipment but also with the long-range nature of the information it provides. If the towed array ship has organic ASW helicopters on board, it can prosecute any contacts obtained immediately. Used in conjunction, these equipments provide a most potent anti-submarine combination.

As already noted, another vessel which makes an excellent anti-submarine sonar platform is the submarine itself. In the same way that it can choose its depth and speed to remain concealed from sonar search, it can also optimise them for passive sonar reception, and, if necessary, can use far greater depths than those available to surface deployed sonars. If it does detect an enemy submarine it is in an excellent position to attack. The resulting hunter-killer capability makes anti-submarine operations a prime role for submarines. Such operations may be conducted either alone, or in cooperation with surface ships and/or aircraft. In the latter mode, tactical coordination is dependent on the

FIGURE 4.5   Towed Array Sonar

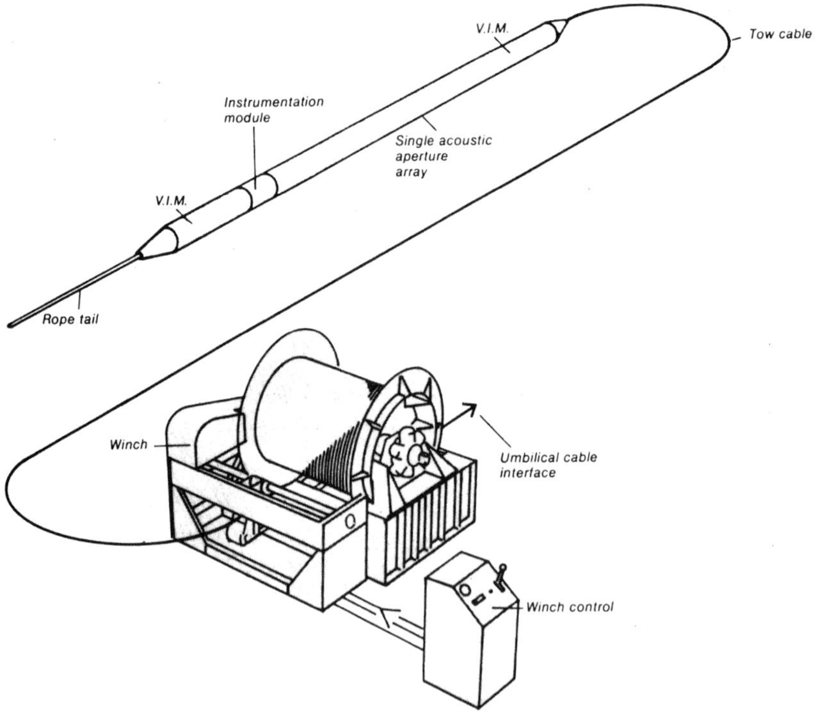

The Plessey COMTASS 1 Towed Array Sonar
(showing acoustic and mechanical components)

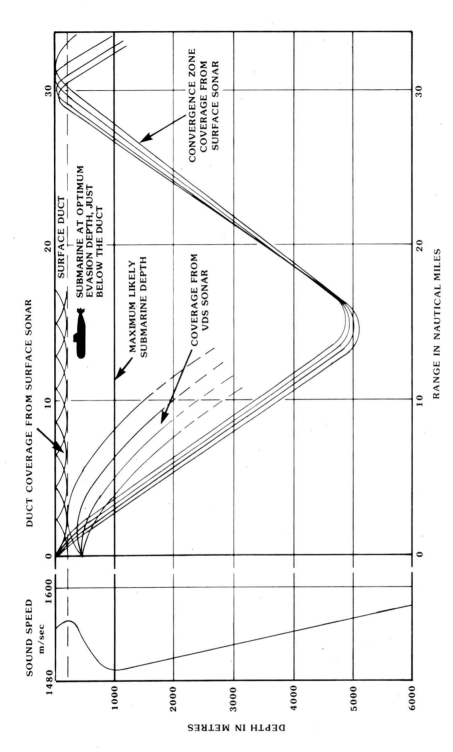

FIGURE 4.6 Tactical use of layers by submarine

ability to communicate with other units via modern submarine equipment such as the towed communications buoy, which is described in the next chapter. Submarines are therefore able to operate in direct support of surface task forces. In view of the need to give them tactical freedom of manoeuvre, and to keep them clear of the noise generated by the task force, submarines employed in this way are likely to be stationed well clear of surface ships, perhaps using aircraft or helicopters to provide a communications link with the force commander.

Underwater Ocean Surveillance

Sonars may be installed on the sea bed as fixed devices, and can then be used to monitor the waters around them for submarine movement. Bottom-mounted sonars may be placed to provide a detecting screen near harbour entrances, in narrow waters such as straits or the mouths of fjords, or in deep ocean to cover transit routes, in particular at the choke points through which submarines must pass to reach their operational areas. As such systems must remain hidden, use minimum electrical power, and provide long detection ranges and wide coverage, the use of the passive mode is obligatory. The undersea surveillance systems obtained by linking such bottom-mounted arrays with computer-controlled facilities ashore provide important intelligence of submarine movements. Nevertheless, compared with the quality of ocean surveillance available from radar and ELINT satellites, underwater surveillance is somewhat patchy, requiring the submarines against which it is targeted to provide the means of detection by emitting noise.

It is of course the SSBN, the nuclear-powered submarine armed with strategic nuclear missiles, that has created the drive on both sides of the Iron Curtain to improve submarine detection and surveillance. Intense research is carried out into other forms of underwater sensors, such as the detection of the infra-red scars on the ocean surface caused by wakes or the welling up of hot water discharges from submarine cooling equipment. However, at present the submarine remains invulnerable to reliable detection by any means other than the use of sound with all its limitations and vagaries, and there is at the moment no sign of any scientific break-through in detection techniques.

Command and Control in Underwater Warfare

The exercise of command and control requires two basic elements; information on the situation, and the ability to communicate. Viewed from this aspect, underwater warfare divides into two domains—the offensive battle conducted by submarines, directed and coordinated from ashore: and the anti-submarine battle, the main components of which are ships and aircraft organised and commanded in tactical groups at sea, but requiring direction and support from ashore. Let us consider first how the submarine captain views his task.

A submarine is a loner, acting by itself, relying on remaining hidden until ready to attack, and then achieving tactical surprise. This is true whether it is nuclear or diesel powered, and whether its mission is to attack shipping or to mount a strategic nuclear deterrent by maintaining a silent patrol with missiles at notice. For such purposes the underwater environment is ideal, indeed this is what has enabled the potential of the modern submarine to be fully exploited. On the whole, a submarine captain has a good picture of the waters around him. He will use passive sonar only, unless he is forced to switch to the active mode in self-defence or for the final stages of attack. Passive sonar will give him very reasonable surveillance of his tactical area, in particular of any ships that are moving at or above cruising speed—say 16 knots—and excellent long-range warning of any that are proceeding at 25 knots or higher. Not only will passive sonar detect such contacts but it will provide a nearly instantaneous classification. His picture will be improved if he can use his optimum operating depth, since he can use the thermal layers to his advantage. When necessary, he can go to the appropriate depth to conceal the submarine from searching ships or aircraft, for example to place the submarine beneath a layer which effectively puts him beyond sonar reach. The submarine can do this without undue risk provided it remains at silent speed, say below four knots; this keeps its own noise down, thus avoiding creating a target for enemy passive sonar, and minimising its own platform noise so that its own sonar efficiency remains high. The only operational penalty that the submarine captain must accept for such advantage is to deny himself the ability to move at higher speeds.

Of course, there will be occasions when the use of high approach speeds cannot be avoided. For example, if the line and speed of advance of the target will not bring it sufficiently close to the submarine's position. In such cases speeds of up to 25 knots or more may have to be used to gain ground and place the submarine in an advantageous position for attack. In these circumstances, the balance of advantage will narrow and may even reverse. By proceeding at high speed, the submarine will become easily detectable and its own sonar picture will be severely degraded by its own noise. In particular, it will become vulnerable to helicopters, alerted by its noisy progress, moving rapidly into its approach path and using passive sonar to track it, unknown to the submarine.

PLATE 4.4   HMS *Dreadnought*, the Royal Navy's first nuclear powered hunter-killer submarine (SSN), entering harbour. Notice the raised periscopes and masts, with aerials and other sensor devices mounted on top. (*Crown Copyright/RN photograph*)

Whatever the mode of approach, the submarine captain may wish to improve his tactical picture before firing his torpedoes or air-flight missiles at ship targets and may then expose a radar aerial or periscope. This will expose the submarine to detection, either visually or by ESM, although these dangers can be minimised by keeping the time of exposure to an absolute minimum and transmitting only a few radar pulses. Despite these difficulties in approaching and attacking ship targets, the submarine retains many advantages and poses a formidable threat.

Where the submarine is penalised by the underwater environment is in the matter of communications. Since it acts alone, the submarine is fortunate in not requiring a pattern of tactical communications, as needed by surface task forces. However, to communicate with his shore authority the submarine captain must use radio. The dangers and difficulties involved and the way in which command and control procedures are tailored to allow the submarine to retain as much tactical freedom as possible, are described in later chapters.

By contrast, compared with their submarine adversaries, the problems faced by commanders of surface task forces and convoy escorts are largely reversed. Radio communication, although vulnerable to enemy EW and requiring complex organisation, is freely available. However, the surveillance picture of the underwater scenario is often incomplete and unreliable. Ships of a task force must usually travel at speed to fulfil their mission; this creates noise which reveals their presence many tens of miles away to listening submarines. These, if advantageously positioned, may then be able to close in at slow or medium speed without exposing themselves. Such pre-positioning of enemy submarines ahead of the force may have been possible from advanced warning of its movements from satellite surveillance. If a submarine is equipped with medium-range anti-ship missiles it may not have to break through the anti-submarine screen in order to attack, perhaps being able to obtain the information it needs to identify its target and direct its weapon from the use of passive sonar, backed up in the later stages of approach by ESM. In such circumstances the first that the surface task force commander will know of his adversary's presence will be an ESM warning of the missile homing radar, and the problem of defence becomes an above-water matter as discussed in other chapters. This is the worst case, but it illustrates the tactical advantage enjoyed by a modern submarine. Even where the latter must use high speed to approach and attack with torpedoes, and thus expose itself to prior detection, the time available to the surface force to take effective counter-action is very limited.

5

Naval Communications

THE eminent American naval historian Alfred Thayer Mahan wrote at the turn of the century 'Communications dominate war . . . they are the most important single element in strategy.' More prosaically, an American general, Mark Clark, remarked during World War II that without communications all he could command was his desk. Mahan would have been aware of the development of radio communications, known then as wireless telegraphy or W/T, but he could hardly have foreseen the impact of the new technology on naval operations. He was probably thinking more about the limitations imposed on naval strategy and tactics by the methods available before Signor Marconi's revolution.

Consider the situation before the 20th century ushered in the radio age. Orders from Admiralty were issued in writing before ships sailed, and remained in force until fresh directions were received by despatch vessel. The chief means of communications between ships at sea was by flag hoist, which necessitated using a signal code limited to set piece manoeuvres and a slow vocabulary. Although shuttered lantern was available, it was only usable at night until the electric lamp was introduced at the end of the 19th century. In any event, these visual methods depended on the eye and telescope and were thus of limited range, a few miles at most. Admirals wishing to acquaint their captains of their plans and intentions in battle had to call a conference in the flagship. This system involved delays that seem incredible today. To work at all, the situation required comprehensive delegation and a good appreciation of one's senior's mind. Much could and did go wrong. To quote one example: in 1781 Admiral Rodney failed to achieve an overwhelming victory over the French at the Battle of Martinique, despite having manoeuvred the British fleet into a dominant position, because his captains did not understand his intended tactics and, fearing his irascible nature, had not questioned him in the pre-battle conference.

Nowadays the situation is almost reversed. As we shall see, the ability to communicate has led to a position where some of the lessons of the past, such as the use of a sensible degree of delegation, and brevity in communication, are in danger of being lost. No one supposes, however, that the advantages of radio should be thrown away. They have transformed the way in which navies are used and fleets directed. We shall be looking in this chapter at the main features of modern naval communications which have created this situation. For simplicity it is based on the Royal Navy.

THE NAVAL COMMUNICATIONS SYSTEM

Naval communications are provided by a wide variety of equipment and facilities, centrally organised by the Ministry of Defence to provide a carefully planned service which enables:

Naval units to be deployed, directed and supported world wide.
Ships and aircraft operating as organised units to coordinate their tactics and the use of their weapons.
Shore-based authorities and establishments to support the fleet.

The central principle on which resources are operated is that of common usage; there are very few dedicated naval communications channels. Equipment such as transmitters and receivers, aerial systems, teleprinters and switching facilities are sited as far as possible together in radio stations or communication centres and then connected, as needed, to provide the circuits and networks required at the time. This is both economical and efficient. Communication configurations must continually be kept up to date as the nature and location of naval deployments and operations change. The pooling of resources allows equipment to be used to the best advantage and provides efficient coverage for breakdowns and war damage.

The principle is taken a step further with the long-distance circuits linking the Ministry of Defence and Commands. The resources required are provided by all three Services and operated as a single system known as the Defence Communications Network (DCN). This is under the operational control of a Controller with a joint staff, who is responsible for its efficiency to the MOD; all three Services use it as required. The DCN is connected via gateway channels to similar national military networks such as the American AUTODIN, and also to the NATO Integrated Communications System (NICS). All such networks and their linked national facilities are operated in accordance with common NATO procedures; the resulting world-wide system enables naval ships and authorities to inter-communicate rapidly and efficiently across the Alliance. In a later section we shall be looking in detail at the radio and satellite circuits required to communicate with ships at sea and the shorter range radio circuits needed within a force.

Setting up radio and communications equipment, routing message traffic and operating message handling equipment are specialised tasks requiring trained communications personnel. However, naval communications are provided to be used by non-communications personnel, from the admiral and his staff to the stores petty officer. The system is accessed by users in three ways: by the use of speech, for example the telephone, so that the users communicate directly to recipients; by the writing of messages, which are then accepted into the system and delivered to recipients as hard copy; and by the exchange of computer data, by the operation of computer controls.

In the United Kingdom much use is made of the telephone by naval users and the public system is used as far as practicable. In addition, there is a government-wide secure speech network which provides a crypto-protected telephone service for all government ministries and the three Services. Satellite circuits are used to extend the system to ships at sea, to link senior officers and their staffs to MOD and other headquarters. Extensive use was made of this relatively new facility during the mounting and conduct of the Falklands Campaign. No other form of communication is as good as a telephone conversation for dealing with complicated subjects or difficult decisions. This is partly because, as we all know, both meaning and nuance can be conveyed by speech in a way that is impossible in written communication. Of equal importance, in a telephone conversation lasting a few minutes, points can be made and answered immediately; to achieve a similar result by exchange of written message would take many hours and still be less effective. The long-distance radio telephone used to be regarded with suspicion by some naval officers since it threatened the freedom of action that they had always enjoyed at sea. However, today the secure telephone connecting the force commander at sea with his commander-in-chief ashore is regarded as both normal and necessary.

Ashore, the telephone is commonplace. At sea, the radio voice circuit is the most commonly met speech facility, being used to direct aircraft, to coordinate the use of weapons, to pass tactical command and manoeuvring signals, and to communicate with tugs and port authorities—to mention only some of its many applications. The normal configuration is the radio net, with all equipment operating on a common frequency. Every transmission is heard by all stations on net, which requires good circuit discipline if communications are not to be jammed by two stations transmitting at once.

The naval logistics and support system in the United Kingdom is nowadays fully computerised, and this requires data circuits between depots, dockyards, headquarters and computer bureaux. The CRISP network links all these computer users, and allows data and instructions to be passed between them at very high speed; as with telephones, satellites enable such circuits to be extended to ships afloat. We shall be looking at the tactical use of data links and explore the general use of computers themselves for command and control in the next chapter.

Signal Messages

Access to the communications system by means of written message and hard copy still represents the most commonly used naval method. It is available to any serviceman or civilian in the Navy ashore or afloat. A message may be originated by anyone with a need, but junior personnel must obtain the authority of a senior Releasing Officer before it is taken to the communications centre for transmission. Signal messages, to use the NATO term, are known throughout the Royal Navy simply as 'signals'.

A signal is the naval equivalent of a telex, with some important differences. It is written on a printed message form, see Figure 5.1. The format is standard throughout NATO and the Western Alliance, and is an important element of the common procedure referred to above. Like the telex, a signal has an address and a text, and names the sender. However the address allows multiple addressees, that is the signal may go to more than one nominated ship or authority and there are two classes of addressee, those for action and those for information. The name of the originator is also part of the address. This sophistication of the

FIGURE 5.1   Naval Message Form

MESSAGE FORM

		Serial No.	F. Sigs. 266
			(Revised AUG. 81)

LINE 1

LINE 2

LINE 3   DE

LINE 4

ROUTING INDICATORS

Precedence-Action	Precedence-Info	DTG, Month, Year
	Routine	

CHECK BOX   (Pads of 100)

Routed by ....

Time ....

Perforated by..................

Time ....

For SINGLE TRANSMISSION

FROM

TO

Transmitted to.................

Channel No/System ....

Time ....

Operator.......................

INFO

MESSAGE INSTRUCTIONS

SECURITY CLASSIFICATION
(Messages referring to a classified message must be classified RESTRICTED or above.)

GR

SIC

INTERNAL DISTRIBUTION

FILE / OR
NUMBER / REFERENCE

DRAFTER'S NAME
IN BLOCK LETTERS

Page............
of
............Pages

refers to a classified message ☐
This message (tick appropriate box)
does not refer to a classified message ☐

TELEPHONE NUMBER	BRANCH
RELEASING OFFICER'S SIGNATURE	RANK

FOR OPR'S USE   R

FILING TIME / TOR	SYSTEM	OPERATOR	FINAL CHECK OPERATOR	NAME IN BLOCK LETTERS

PRINTED IN THE U.K. FOR HMSO, 8410056, 1/85. 2137

(Crown Copyright)

address is important since it widens the scope and meaning of a signal. An example of a short operational signal, ordering two ships to leave one Task Unit and join another, is shown in Figure 5.2. Notice how the address makes it clear that the two ships are to act as indicated, and at the same time informs the Task Force Commander and both Task Unit commanders of what the Task Group Commander has ordered. Multiple addressees of a signal mean that when the signal form reaches the originator's communication centre further work must be done on it before transmission, to ensure that it is routed to all ships and authorities included in the address.

An important feature of the naval signal system is that signals are deemed to be addressed to the senior officer of the unit named. An extension of the principle is that signals to Flag Officers are addressed to them, not their headquarters. In the illustrative signal it is the captains of HMS *Graceful* and HMS *Flourish* who are addressed, not just two amorphous entities represented by the ships' names. This sharpens the system, as it leaves no doubt where orders are directed and responsibility lies. If it is necessary to communicate only with a particular officer, the signal is addressed to his ship or establishment and the first words of the text indicate his name or title (eg 'For Principal Medical Officer'). However, over-use of this method of private communication is frowned on since it tends to bypass the proper staff procedures.

There are other constituents of a naval signal that are not part of a telex. The originator must indicate the security classification, and the precedence. The same security classifications that are employed in letters and documents are used; this ensures that the correct cryptographic protection is given to a signal during transmission and that it is handled correctly during all stages of its life. As to precedence, the markings used are Routine, Priority, Immediate and Flash. The precedence marking on a naval signal indicates the degree of urgency, not its deemed importance, nor the rank of the originator as is the procedure in some armies. The use of precedence during transmission, to ensure that the most urgent signals get through first, is discussed below. Last but not least, every signal carries a date-time group (DTG) indicating its time of origination, which also serves as its reference.

Finally, of course, the text. Traditionally, naval signals are conducted as short and pungent repartee. It is good to report that the art form is alive and well and thriving in the Royal Navy. To quote a modern example, not many years ago a destroyer was in collision with the flagship in the North Atlantic. As the vessels drew slowly apart in the oily swell the admiral signalled 'What are you going to do now?' Quick as a flash came the reply 'Buy a farm'.

On a more serious note the ability to convey meaning clearly and concisely is of enormous practical value. It keeps a signal short, thus reducing the time needed to both transmit and read it. More importantly it avoids misunderstandings. There is a strong belief in the Navy that the discipline of having to express thoughts and orders in the form of a concise written message results in clear direction and positive response. The signal illustrated in Figure 5.2 is an example of clarity and brevity, which allows no doubt about what is required and who is to do it. There are conventions which assist. Flowery, and thus ambiguous, words are normally avoided, and established professional terminology used to the maximum. Signals have coined their own vocabulary, in many cases the heritage of the precision of the codes associated with the earlier use of flags. Space does not permit elaboration, but one example will illustrate the point. The terms 'intend' and 'propose' have much the same meaning in everyday use ashore. However to the Navy they are quite distinct. 'Propose' means making a suggestion for one's superior to agree and authorise. The correct reply is either 'Approved' or 'Not approved'. In contradistinction, the term 'intend' signifies that the originator will carry out the action unless ordered not to.

The previous paragraph discussed messages of a tactical command nature, most of which will be dictated by the senior officers themselves or drafted by their staff. However, much signal traffic is far longer, sometimes necessarily so. Intelligence reports, stores requests, administrative instructions to quote only some, do not lend themselves to short, neat texts. Routine messages may be reduced in length by the use of standard formats. Not only is this shorter and often easier to use, it also means that, as the format must be completed, nothing is forgotten. There is another advantage in using formats: they enable the information in the signal to be injected into computers with the minimum of reprocessing. In fact this has now become a necessity when communicating with any senior officer whose headquarters is equipped with CCIS, such as discussed in the next chapter. As with so many other aspects of communications, formats and formating have become a matter requiring international standardisation, and here the procedural document is known as Allied Data Publication No 3 (ADatP3). This lays down formats for virtually every sort of message and subject and, in several ways, resembles the old signal codes. The result is a signal that is both man and machine readable. One of the benefits to command and control is that the standard opening sections of each signal require the position, course and speed to be stated if originated from a ship at sea, thus providing a regular check without extra signalling. It seems likely that this type of formated message will gradually supersede older methods.

FIGURE 5.2   Example of Short Operational Signal

TO: GRACEFUL   FROM: CTG 678.1

       FLOURISH   310706Z OCT

INFO: CTF 678   IMMEDIATE

       CTU 678.1.1

       CTU 678.1.3

- -

CONFIDENTIAL.   GRACEFUL TAKE FLOURISH UNDER HIS ORDERS AND DETACH FROM

TU 678.1.1 AT 311200Z IN ACCORDANCE WITH OPERATION BANNOCK ANNEX CHARLIE (7),

PROCEEDING WEST OF FOUL ISLAND TO JOIN TU 678.1.3 BY 311800Z.

LONG-RANGE RADIO COMMUNICATIONS

Let us now look at the means by which naval communications serve ships at sea. The only primary method available is radio, either direct, via the ionosphere, or by the use of satellites. Visual signalling, although a useful secondary method within a force, is limited to horizon range.

High-Frequency Broadcasts and Ship-Shore

The most demanding technical requirement is long-range communication between ships and the shore. In the past, this has been possible only by means of High-Frequency (HF) radio, and this is still used extensively. The HF technique uses the phenomenon known as refraction to 'bounce' radio waves off the ionosphere, thus allowing communication to occur around the earth's curvature over many hundreds of miles. In practice one bounce (ie 'single hop' communication) is more reliable than several (known as 'multi-hop'), and HF radio services are therefore arranged so that, as far as possible, transmitters and receivers are separated by no more than a thousand miles or so. Communication from shore to ship is provided by high-power multi-frequency broadcasts, whereby several transmitters, each using a different frequency, are keyed simultaneously. This provides ships at sea with a choice of frequency for reception, a vital feature which enables the ship to optimise reception for the prevailing conditions. (As explained below, the suite of transmitters for this purpose may include one LF transmitter as well as several HF ones.) A well planned multi-frequency broadcast of this type therefore provides, under normal propagation conditions, unbroken and reliable area coverage; traffic schedules are organised so that ships can read it without having to transmit to acknowledge receipt. The reverse path from ship to shore is provided by inverting the arrangement, the shore station maintaining receiving watch on a number of frequencies, and ships selecting the optimum transmission frequency.

Sometimes a direct HF ship-shore-ship circuit is established between a flagship and a shore radio station, known as a Maritime Rear Link (MRL). As only two stations are on net the frequencies can be adjusted to suit their distance apart and the time of day. Most traffic is to and from flagships, so an MRL serves the primary route well. Other traffic for the remainder of the force is then relayed to other ships. This may well be routed via an HF Task Force broadcast, transmitted by the flagship to all ships of the force, using procedures similar to the shore-ship broadcasts described above.

High-Frequency communication is simple and inexpensive but it has a number of serious disadvantages. It is not totally reliable, being prone to man-made interference and ionospheric disturbance and capable of being disrupted by high level nuclear explosions. The HF frequency spectrum is limited in extent, which restricts the number of available communication channels. These are, in any event, of limited capacity and not suitable for most types of data transmission. The use of HF will probably reveal the position of the transmitter as it is easy to DF from long range; this debars its use at sea in many war situations. Finally, HF is no longer an attractive method of providing a reliable, high-capacity, world-

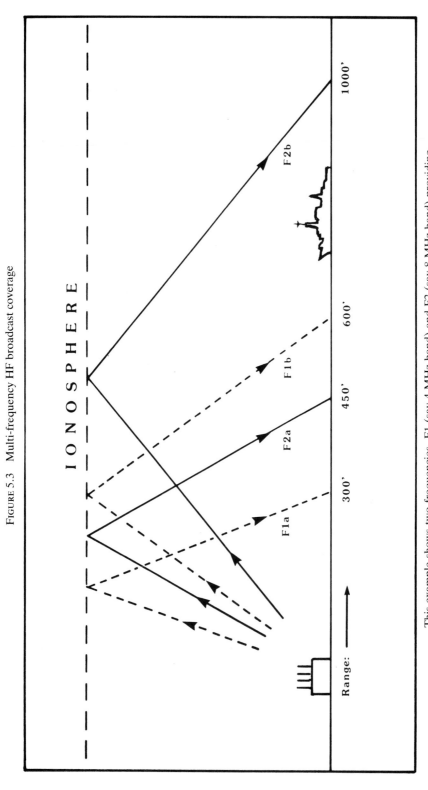

FIGURE 5.3 Multi-frequency HF broadcast coverage

This example shows two frequencies, F1 (say 4 MHz band) and F2 (say 8 MHz band) providing overlapping coverage from 300 to 1000 miles from transmitters.

F1 is receivable from 300 to 600 miles range.
F2 is receivable from 450 to 1000 miles.
F1 and F2 are receivable from 450 to 600 miles.

wide communications system, since this would require what, in these days, would be an impracticable number of carefully separated shore radio stations. The limitations of HF have in fact provided a strong incentive for the development of the naval use of satellite communications (Satcom) as the new primary system. Nevertheless, despite its disadvantages, HF provides the only fallback method of long-distance naval communication, on which command and control would have to rely were the satellite system to fail.

Satellite Communications

Most satellite communication systems use geo-stationary space craft. The systems discussed in this chapter are of that type. The satellite is placed in a west-to-east orbit about 23,000 miles above the equator, at which height its angular velocity is the same as the earth's rotation. To the observer on earth it therefore appears to be stationary, with the advantage of avoiding the need for automatic tracking. A satellite 23,000 miles above the equator can be 'seen' from the earth's surface within a large circular area centred on the equator. If the centre is on the Greenwich meridian, the East-West extremities will be approximately 65E and 65W, and the North-South extremities 70N and 70S. This area is known as the satellite's 'footprint'. The actual limits are determined by the ability of ships' equipment to receive effective signals at very low angles of altitude, at which point the satellite would, if it were visible, appear like a star near the horizon. The footprint reaches, typically, from Iceland in the Northern Hemisphere to well south of Cape Horn in the Southern. It requires three correctly positioned geo-stationary satellites to provide overlapping coverage of the world's oceans, between the tropics of Cancer and Capricorn.

Considerations of cost, in particular the satellites themselves, place a practical limit on the number of systems available. Currently, two major satcom systems are of significance to the navies of NATO and the Western Alliance. The most extensive of these is the American Defense Satellite Communications System (DSCS), which operates in the SHF region of the frequency band. The British 'Skynet' satellites are built to similar specifications and are interoperable with DSCS, as also are NATO owned equivalents. All three sets of satellites are operated on a cooperative basis to the mutual advantage of all parties.

At these frequencies it is necessary to use high-gain dish aerials, which, for warship use, must be stabilised to compensate for ship motion. The SCOT series of British warship terminals, manufactured by Marconi, with their 1 m-2 m dish aerials enclosed in radomes are typical. The twin aerial layout of SCOT is of interest. The aerials are installed so that at least one is always in sight of the satellite, clear of masts and superstructure. This provides SCOT with unbroken transmission and reception, which has always been a feature of radio communication in warships. Without it, vital messages could be lost or delayed at a critical moment and valuable circuit time wasted in having them repeated. SCOT was the first warship satcom system to be fitted with this important facility of unbroken hemispherical coverage. The twin aerials also provide a useful degree of operational redundancy. Since they can be sited relatively low down on the superstructure, they leave the prime masthead sites available for other electronic equipments like radar.

The reliability and capacity of the Skynet and DSCS systems have revolutionised not only naval communications but also command and control and fleet support. Satcom circuits carry reliable high-speed communication channels, which means that message traffic, from command messages to stores requests, arrive more certainly and more rapidly. Traffic to and from ships is usually organised on similar lines to HF broadcasts and ship-shore, as described above, and combinations of these services can be used for Task Force communications. We have already seen that they also allow senior officers to speak by secure telephone with headquarters ashore on important matters, instead of having to

PLATE 5.1 Artist's impression of the UK communication satellite 'SKYNET 4'. The wing-like protrusions are banks of solar cells which power the satellite's controls and payload system. (*Courtesy Marconi*)

rely on interpretation of the written word. In many ways satcoms have effectively integrated the Fleet into the rest of the military and political command system ashore.

The other current naval satcom system is the American Fleet Satellite Communication System (FLTSATCOM). This has been designed on somewhat

PLATE 5.2   HMS *Beaver* with her LYNX helicopter in attendance. The twin radomes of her SCOT satellite communications system can be seen mounted either side on platforms abreast the foremast.
(*Courtesy NAVAL FORCES. Crown Copyright/RN photograph*)

different principles from DSCS, with its relatively sophisticated and expensive shipborne equipment. FLTSATCOM uses the UHF band, and the USN was therefore able to employ relatively simple and proven UHF ship equipment for it, rather than develop a new equipment range, such as was needed for DSCS. Also, as UHF frequencies allowed ships to use simple satcom aerials, a fleet-wide fit was achieved at relatively low cost. The system has been made available to NATO navies for some purposes and the Royal Navy has acquired a limited share of the system's capacity for fleet and submarine use. FLTSATCOM is an excellent system, but it has its shortcomings, notably in the restricted number of channels available and its limited protection against jamming. For this reason, the USN use the DSCS system already described for its larger vessels and command ships.

Finally, mention must be made of the International Maritime Satellite System, INMARSAT. This is a civil system, designed for all types of merchant vessel and associated port and marine facilities. By its charter, it is restricted to use for peaceful purposes. It provides radio telephone and telex services linked to the public networks ashore. Being a civil system, its value for naval purposes is limited. However, it is frequently used by patrol vessels engaged in offshore policing and fishery protection, by warships engaged in peace keeping operations and by naval auxiliaries which are operated as merchant ships.

Coastal and Local Communications

The long-range communications discussed in the previous section serve ships at sea in any region and are not directly linked to any particular flag officer ashore. The radio and satcom stations involved route traffic between ships and head-quarters as necessary. However, in the sea areas around coasts, radio communication is required which is directly connected to and controlled by the local sea area commander or port authority. This gives them the ability to communicate directly with ships operating locally under their command and control, and avoids the complications of routing traffic over the longer-range networks intended for ships further afield. The most frequently used band of radio frequencies for this purpose is Medium Frequency (MF) (See Table 2.1), which has the advantage of providing unbroken coverage out to two hundred miles or so. If longer range is required, the lower frequencies of the HF band can be used to extend this as necessary. Such frequencies are used to establish Local Command Nets and other local circuits for the control of exercises, weapons practice, calibration and range control, and the like, which are guarded by ships in the local areas as appropriate. In the immediate approaches to the naval base, frequencies with much shorter range will suffice. Here the most commonly used band will be the military UHF band 225–400 MHz. Ships in port will keep watch on a number of UHF circuits and may be able to close down completely on HF and MF. Ships alongside in the UK will usually connect to the telephone and teleprinter systems and receive all traffic by this means.

In the United Kingdom, a novel system has recently been introduced to provide coastal communications between operational authorities ashore and ships and maritime aircraft. Named the UK Maritime Coastal Communication

System (UKMACCS), it is operated by the Royal Navy. It introduces a new concept, based on the use of HF skywave and employing frequencies in the lower end of the HF band. Such frequencies provide excellent and reliable communication at medium range but will frequently suffer a dead zone nearer the transmitter. The full technical reasons for this would require a lengthy explanation but, briefly, the ionospheric 'bounce' mechanism illustrated in Figure 5.3 has, for each frequency, a minimum range of refraction, inside which the frequency will not propagate back to earth. (This minimum range of return is known as the 'skip distance'.) UKMACCS exploits this principle by using transmitter and receiver sites in both the north and the south, which serve, respectively, ships and aircraft in the south, and in the north. This ensures that ships and aircraft are separated from the radio stations they are working with by several hundreds of miles, and that no mobile unit is placed in the dead zone. Ships and aircraft inter-operate with whichever radio station provides the best communications path.

An important group of communications relate to the Navy's responsibility for coordinating rescue and emergency services in support of offshore activities such as oil and gas rigs, and in fishery protection, which is an important role for Sea Area Commanders in the United Kingdom. Essentially, this means that the Navy must be able to use civil frequencies and procedures, since the miscellany of civilian craft and installations forming what is known colloquially as 'the Offshore Tapestry' will not be able to use naval systems. In many cases it will just be a matter of re-tuning equipment provided for naval purposes to the appropriate international or civil frequency and working without crypto-protection. Most naval equipments have this capability. Where a commonly used civil band is not covered by naval equipment, the Navy may have to fit civil equipment for the purpose; a good example is the channels in the International Maritime Mobile VHF FM Band (156–174 MHz), equipment for which is carried by all merchant ships, fishing craft and similar vessels. This is such an important facility that the Navy fits it anyway. Another example is the INMARSAT Satellite service,

PLATE 5.3   HMS *Jersey*, a British 'Island' Class offshore patrol vessel, with an oil platform in the background. These warships must communicate regularly with civilian ships and installations. (*Courtesy NAVAL FORCES. Crown Copyright/RN photograph*)

discussed above; however these terminals are bulky and can be installed only at the expense of other naval equipment.

Providing equipment that enables direct working with merchant ships has other bonuses. Such equipment is likely to be required for convoy communications, and will also provide warships with the ability to take part in search and rescue (SAR) and disaster relief anywhere in the world.

Maritime Aircraft

Maritime aircraft operating from air bases ashore also need communications to link them with their controlling authorities, with cooperating ships and with their airfields on return. Long-range communications are usually provided, using high frequency on an area basis, rather like those for ships in a local sea area, with careful choice of transmitter and radio frequency to provide complete radio coverage. Maritime aircraft cooperating with ships will use short-range circuits in the UHF band when within range, and MF or frequencies in the low end of the HF band when beyond the reach of UHF.

TASK FORCE COMMUNICATIONS

The long-range HF and satcom systems described above are ship-shore-ship services. Their function is to connect ships to shore headquarters and the shore-based facilities. They may also be used by ships to communicate with other ships, messages being relayed via inter-connecting networks as necessary but, with the important exception of a Task Force broadcast, they are not intended to provide primary links between vessels of a force at sea. Naval operations usually involve groups of mixed vessels to provide a balanced force, and the tactical command and control of such forces presents demanding communications requirements. The task force will probably be disposed over a large ocean area, the main elements being within a broad circle of about 100 miles radius. Inside this tactical area, a number of groups will be operating in close formations, while single ships will be acting as pickets on the periphery or further out. The radio communications circuits serving a task force therefore fall into two broad categories, depending on the range over which they are required to carry. Close formations can use 'Line of Sight' radio, which reaches to the radio horizon, which in the case of inter-ship communications is of the order of 15–20 miles, depending on the sizes of the ships concerned and thus the heights of their aerials. For communication with pickets, and between formed groups, it will be necessary to use 'Extended Line of Sight'—also known as 'Over the Horizon'—radio, which will carry out to 200–300 miles.

Line of Sight (LOS) radio circuits in a naval formation are normally in the UHF frequency band (225–400 MHz) which was developed after World War II for military communications. LOS circuits provide short-range communications for the control of manoeuvring, aircraft and helicopter direction, the control and coordination of weapons and tactics, and the reporting of information obtained from ships' sensors. Their range is similar to the maximum range of detection shown in Table 2.4, and they are also affected by 'anaprop' in the same ways as radar, as discussed in Chapter 2. A large number of LOS circuits are needed for the tactical control of a mixed force. Most operate on the principle of the voice radio net, in which all stations are tuned to the same frequency for transmission and reception. Only one station can transmit at a time and all stations receive what is being transmitted. This has the advantages of technical simplicity, and it means that everyone on net hears all traffic and thus knows what is going on. UHF radio is normally clear of static, so communication is good and, as we shall see later, its short range has advantages for security. The disadvantages of UHF net radio are that it requires strict procedural discipline to avoid mutual interference from two or more stations transmitting together. Because only one station can transmit at a time, its capacity is limited. The other type of LOS circuit operated between ships is the data link, which automatically connects tactical computer systems at a high data rate. Data links are fast becoming an essential feature of modern naval warfare; without them tactical computers cannot develop their full potential, which stems in large measure from their ability to intercommunicate with one another, thus sharing information and allowing weapon control orders to be passed automatically. They are discussed in the next chapter.

Extended Line of Sight (ELOS) circuits are usually provided by Medium Frequencies (MF) or frequencies in the lower end of the HF band. These frequencies will propagate beyond the horizon to about 300 miles, but beyond that will normally be attenuated, with the advantage of not carrying to a listening enemy. The functions of such circuits are similar to those of the LOS circuits already discussed and they are operated as radio nets or data links. In the case of pickets equipped with sensors requiring a high-capacity circuit for the trans-mission of data, which would normally be beyond the scope of MF/HF circuits, resort must be made either to aircraft relay using UHF frequencies, or communi-cating via a suitable satellite communications system.

The Task Force commander will need to have good communication with all units in his TF and will probably establish a task force broadcast, keyed by the flagship for this purpose and using similar procedures to the shore-ship broad-casts discussed above. The TF broadcast will be supported by a TF calling circuit for ships to pass messages in to the flagship. These circuits may be HF or MF, but in modern conditions ships may read a satcom broadcast channel as TF broadcast, keyed by the TF commander using another satcom channel, and backed by further satcom channels to provide a calling circuit. This illustrates the flexibility of the satcom system. In addition to its reliability, such an arrangement avoids ships transmitting on HF with all its associated disadvantages, as dis-cussed elsewhere in this book.

An important development in Task Force communications will occur during the next decade or so, as a new system of communication is introduced for LOS and ELOS circuits. This is known as 'multi-functional information distribution', and is exemplified by the American Joint Tactical Information Distribution System (JTIDS). The system is, in effect, an automatic data link, operating in D Band (see Table 2.3). The technical and operational standards associated with its operation are known as Link 16; transmission is by high-speed data. The system is nominally LOS in nature but, as it is intended to be relayed automatically by aircraft, this effectively extends its range well beyond horizon range for ship-to-ship use, thereby making it ELOS in this mode. The basic facility is to link computers, as a data link, but also to carry some channels of conventional communication. One of its novel features is that it incorporates a degree of automatic protection against jamming, giving it 'ECM resistance'. It also provides relative position, as discussed in Chapter 2. JTIDS is an expensive system and it will not be universally fitted in all warships. Carriers, guided missile ships and pickets are the likely recipients, together with AEW aircraft and fighters. The RAF will be fitting this system for the UK Air Defence Region, and there should therefore be an interoperable channel with naval task forces similarly equipped.

Communications Planning

We have already examined the central principle of naval communications provision, namely the pooling of shore-based equipment. This is applied with equal force afloat. All ship communication equipment, however specialised in function, is sited together in radio rooms and communications centres. This is placed under the control of the communications officer, who is responsible to the captain that it is used to the best advantage to meet current commitments. The

PLATE 5.4   British minesweepers deploy for peace-keeping operations in the Gulf. Notice the INMARSAT terminal fitted for the deployment on the afterdeck. (*Courtesy MOD Navy/Crown Copyright*)

resulting statement of how equipment is to be set-up and connected is known as the Communications Plan (or Complan). One of the complications is that complete flexibility is not possible. Ships' equipment such as transmitters, receivers, and aerials can be set only to certain combinations of frequencies (which vary from ship to ship), and connected in certain ways. This is partly due to the technical design of the actual equipment, and partly to the problem known as electromagnetic compatibility or EMC. With so much radio equipment operating within narrow confines of a warship, mutual interference, caused by unwanted electrical interactions, is difficult to avoid. Although the primary problem concerns communications equipment only, EMC knows no departmental boundary; for example, ECM equipment can jam satcoms and UHF equipment can disrupt radar. The solution lies in using compatible combinations of equipment, and avoiding the simultaneous use of systems known to cause unacceptable mutual interference.

During extended operations in war, the Complan will alter relatively infrequently, as each phase unfolds. However, in peacetime exercises, such phases are often of artifically short duration, in order to extract maximum operational value in the time available. Thus each phase may necessitate adjustments to the Complan. The planning and overall supervision of the communications organisation is one of the principal duties of senior communications specialists, usually middle rank officers on fleet, force and ship staffs. They carry considerable responsibility, since defective planning may result in widespread failure of communications, with severe operational consequences.

Interoperability

A further and more fundamental problem is the difficulty of providing an adequate degree of communications interoperability. To link all units of a force, radio transmissions must be capable of being transmitted and received by all. This is simple where identical equipment is fitted, but that is not always possible. Ships are constructed at different times, and brand new radio equipment will be installed, only on building, in a small proportion of the Fleet. Retrofitting is very expensive and uses scarce resources that are then not available for other purposes. Retrofit can therefore only be used for the most essential communications equipment. Even then, since most systems must be installed during formal refitting periods, it will take several years before a fleet-wide fit is achieved.

The problem is worse in NATO, where ships of different nationality are even less likely to have identical equipment. If one radio is to operate with another, non-identical but serving a similar purpose, they must use common technical standards. This may sound simple, and indeed NATO has an active programme pursuing this objective. However, in many cases, there are valid reasons why it is not practicable for international standards to be adopted, remembering that ships have to communicate with their own national units and systems. Moreover, as a new standard will need to be retrofitted, or included in new builds, it will take years for it to be introduced across all navies of the Alliance. The general effect has been made worse by the increasing degree of equipment specialisation, and by the advent of digital techniques and data processing, which has added the complication of software. The problem of providing a satisfactory level of interoperability within the NATO Navies is a continuing one, which is unlikely to ease while systems become ever more complex. The results at sea often represent a direct problem to command and control, because unless there is an adequate degree of communications interoperability within a force of mixed nationalities it will be impossible to effect satisfactory tactical coordination.

SUBMARINE COMMUNICATIONS

As with surface ships, the only practicable method of long-range communication with submarines is by radio. Underwater communication by sound is possible but, as we have seen earlier, is very restricted in range and can be used only between a submarine and cooperating units in the immediate vicinity. This introduces great complication, as it means that, in order to communicate, the submarine must expose an aerial above the surface, involving interference with its freedom of manoeuvre. Submarine communications, and the related command and control procedures, are therefore very carefully tailored to permit the submarine captain as much tactical freedom as practicable, whilst still guaranteeing that essential communication will occur.

Radio waves, with one important exception, will not penetrate sea water. The exception is the band of frequencies at the very bottom of the spectrum, known as Low, Very Low and Extremely Low Frequencies (LF, VLF and ELF). A high-power VLF broadcast transmitted from shore can be read by a submerged submarine when shallow at ranges out to 1000 miles or more, depending on the radiated power. This provides a reliable channel of communication for passing information and orders to the submarine without it having to break surface. The method is not ideal since the need to come to shallow depth restricts the captain's choice of operating depth. As we have seen, a submarine needs to be able to select its operating depth in order to optimise sonar conditions, and the need to go shallow could result, for instance, in breaking contact with a target. Transmission on a VLF broadcast is therefore organised so that as far as possible the submarine captain can choose the time to come up to read signal traffic. Messages for each submarine reading the broadcast are serially numbered and transmitted in batches at set times known as routines. These are repeated, so that if a submarine misses one routine it can use a subsequent one. This gives the submarine captain considerable freedom, but it means that his HQ ashore cannot be certain when a message addressed to a submarine has actually reached it.

VLF has other disadvantages. Due to the small bandwidth at such low frequencies signal transmission is restricted to slow telegraph speeds, and despite recent improvements to increase the number of channels on each carrier frequency it remains the case that VLF broadcast capacity is limited. There is also a shortage of available radio frequencies in this small and congested band, which limits the number of VLF broadcasts that can serve a given theatre of operations. Finally, VLF transmitter stations are large and expensive installations which take years to plan and build. However, despite the drawbacks a VLF broadcast is an effective and reliable method of communicating from shore to submarine; it is therefore, where available, the primary means of shore to submarine communications.

ELF provides a specialised communications facility. At such frequencies the data rate is very slow, and normal communication by means of teleprinter is not practicable. However the method gives very long range and reception is possible at greater depths than with VLF; ELF is also extremely reliable and difficult to disrupt. It is used for the passing of vital coded command messages, such as nuclear weapon control. ELF transmitters and their associated aerials are vast and very expensive installations, owing to the wavelengths involved, which may be tens or hundreds of miles long and thus require aerials of similar scale.

What neither ELF nor VLF can do is to provide a reciprocal communications path from submarine to shore. Although only needed infrequently, when it is required it becomes essential. Until recently the only method has been HF, and this is still the most widely used. HF will propagate over very long range by sky-wave via the ionosphere and requires relatively low power. However, in order to communicate by this means (and indeed by any radio frequency) the submarine must expose its aerial above the surface. To do so, using conventional aerials, necessitates coming to periscope depth, with the consequential operational penalty. The raising of an aerial exposes it to detection by radar or sighting, although this is a small risk unless enemy units are in the immediate vicinity; moreover the use of reciprocal intercept equipment, as discussed in Chapter 3, will give protection against aircraft radar. Of far greater significance, however, are the risks of actually transmitting. The radio signal can be picked up and DF'd by the enemy intercept service and the position of the submarine compromised. The likelihood of this is high, given the scale and sophistication of modern DF systems. The consequences of transmitting on HF are so drastic that for most submarine operations it is usual to maintain HF silence unless the need to communicate to shore becomes paramount.

The other function of HF radio is to provide a back-up to VLF broadcasts, for use when they are not available or the submarine is beyond their range. As for ships, multi-frequency is used to provide continuous coverage and a message batching system is followed, as for VLF broadcasts. An HF broadcast used in this way will provide a usable substitute for VLF, but its comparative unreliability, coupled with the need to expose an aerial for reception, makes it very much a second best.

Low Frequencies (LF) are also used to provide back-up submarine broadcasts. These frequencies propagate via the ground wave, like VLF, these frequencies can be read by submarines when shallow. The extreme range of LF is much less than VLF and submerged reception is only possible out to a few hundreds of miles from the transmitter. On the other hand LF transmitters are much less expensive than VLF ones and there are more frequencies available. Thus, LF can be used to provide a usable, if second-best, submarine broadcast should VLF fail. Whilst on the subject of LF, it is worth noting that a multi-frequency HF broadcast may carry an LF component, that is an LF transmitter may be keyed simultaneously with the HF transmitters. This widens the choice of received frequency, and provides good, reliable and unbroken reception out to the limit of radio coverage.

PLATE 5.5   HMS *Conqueror*, a nuclear powered hunter-killer submarine. Communications with submarines must be organised to allow them maximum tactical freedom, consistent with positive command and control. (*Courtesy NAVAL FORCES. Crown Copyright/RN photograph*)

Modern Improvements

In recent years there have been a number of improvements to the traditional methods of submarine communications outlined above. These have included the use of on-line crypto-protection, and multi-channelling of VLF to increase capacity. More fundamental methods have been aimed at eliminating, or at least reducing, the operational penalties involved in the submarine communicating with the outside world. The first group of improvements are intended to avoid the problems of the submarine having to come to shallow depth to transmit or receive. One solution involves the submarine streaming a long buoyant wire aerial. This streams astern and upwards, and breaks surface several hundreds metres astern. The end of the wire is used as a receiving aerial. A similar method is to deploy the aerial in a hydrodynamically designed buoy, which is towed on a multi-core cable that also acts as electrical conductor. The positive buoyancy and hydrofoil shape directs the buoy up and it is towed just below the surface some distance astern. These two methods allow the submarine to receive VLF and other bands including HF. The buoy can also contain simple radio equipment, in addition to the aerial system, to enable radio transmission in the HF and higher bands as well as reception. The use of towed devices gives the submarine a means of communicating without having to go to periscope depth and thus allows many operational tasks to continue at the same time. One of the most important advantages is that such devices enable submarines to cooperate with surface ships and aircraft in seeking and hunting enemy submarines. They are not, however, without some penalty. The depths that may be used are not as great as might be desired, and the submarine's freedom to choose its speed and course is restricted. Nevertheless, they are valuable additions to a submarine's communications capability.

Another equipment which enables a submarine to communicate without going shallow is the expendable radio buoy, which contains a radio transmitter and a pre-programmed message. It is ejected whilst the submarine is deep and floats to the surface. Here, either immediately or after a set delay, the aerial is erected and transmission occurs. When transmission is complete, the buoy self-destructs and sinks. This is a most useful device, providing a method of the submarine

FIGURE 5.4   Submarine with Communications Buoy streamed

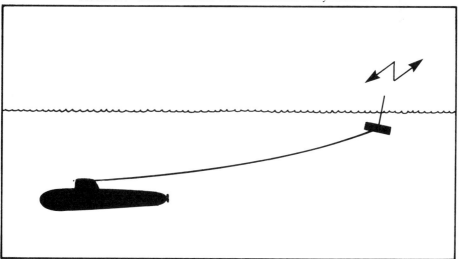

transmitting whilst retaining full tactical freedom. Any frequency band except VLF or LF may be used. Although the transmission may be DF'd the set delay before commencing transmission enables the submarine to open its range from the buoy before its position is compromised. The cost of these buoys is not small, but in scale with their operational value. The only limitation is in the number of buoys that can be carried for one patrol.

The most recent innovation is the extension of satellite communications to submarines. The aerial is mounted on a mast and the submarine must come to periscope depth to communicate. However, the method offers significant advantages over other forms of submarine communication. The radio frequencies are in the UHF band and traffic capacity is therefore far greater than with VLF and HF. This system allows simultaneous transmission and reception at data communication speeds. Traffic management is under computer control; routine periods are used, as with broadcast procedures but, if necessary, a submarine can alert the shore station that it is on the air and have all outstanding traffic for it transmitted, whilst at the same time clearing all its own traffic for shore. This procedure means that there are no set times at which communication must occur, as with VLF routines; moreover, the duration of communication, and thus time at periscope depth, is dramatically reduced, as all outstanding traffic is cleared in both directions within seconds. The operational penalties attached to communicating are therefore greatly reduced, and the communication process itself is far more reliable and rapid. Another advantage is that the MHQ knows when traffic is received by the submarine and, at the same time, has confirmation that it is still safe and well. This method of submarine communications is based on the use of the American FLTSATCOM system, described above; in many ways it has transformed submarine command and control. It was invaluable to RN submarines during the Falklands Campaign.

COMMUNICATIONS PERFORMANCE

The qualities required of naval communications, in order of importance, have been defined for many years as 'Reliability, Security and Speed' and this is still a valid method of assessing performance.

Reliability

The reliability of communications can be defined as the probability of a message arriving uncorrupted at its correct destination, or of a required circuit being available and usable. It is therefore a combination of the reliability of equipment, the quality of radio propagation paths, the ability of the system to withstand enemy countermeasures (particularly jamming) and the extent to which system operation is prone to human error. By these criteria modern naval communications can be given a high mark. Communicators no longer hold their breath to see if capricious equipment will deliver a vital message without letting them down. Modern electronics technology has made communications systems as reliable as the domestic television set and the introduction of digital control has led to precision in equipment setting and a reduction in the vagaries of equipment operation. These technical improvements coupled with high training standards of naval personnel has led to a situation in which equipment failure and human error are rare occurrences. Much the same story applies to radio propagation. Communication by satellite or UHF is inherently reliable, and where necessary is aided by error detection and correction (EDC) equipment. Propagation by HF remains potentially fickle, as the laws of nature have not changed, but even here EDC techniques have greatly improved circuit reliability. In any event, as we have seen, satcoms is generally available as the primary long-distance system.

It would nevertheless be complacent to ignore the extent to which radio communications are open to enemy electronic countermeasures (ECM). As we have seen in Chapter 3 jamming is the main threat; our potential enemies are aware of the effectiveness of this branch of modern warfare, and are well equipped for it. The impending introduction of ECM resistant communications for LOS systems is therefore an important development.

Another grave concern must be the dependence of our command and control system on satellite communications. These are exposed to catastrophic failure through the loss of the satellite or its communications transponder, either by accident or deliberate enemy action. For example, the shuttle disaster illustrated the dependence of satellites on launch systems. Naval communications are undoubtedly very reliable under normal conditions but there must remain a worrying question mark over their capacity in war.

Security

Security of communications in its widest sense covers the protection of communications traffic, whether transmitted by message, voice or data, from interception, D/F and textual analysis by an enemy. In such respects naval communications show great improvements when compared with the past. As regards intercept and D/F, the main changes for the better stem from the increased use of UHF radio and the introduction of satellite communications as a substitute for long-range HF. The frequencies used by both these methods propagate in straight lines, much as light does, and can therefore be intercepted by an enemy only 'in sight' of the transmitter. In the case of UHF circuits the problem is therefore limited to enemy ships and aircraft which are already so close that they are probably already within radar range. In the case of satellite communications, the up-link frequencies transmitted by the ship behave similarly to UHF circuits. An enemy can of course 'see' the space craft, and can therefore intercept the down-link frequencies. These, however, are invariably crypto protected and thus no useful information is available. The principal source of insecurity from enemy intercept and D/F lies in the continuing use of HF for long-range ship-shore, and HF/MF for medium-range ELOS circuits. Since HF ship-shore frequencies propagate over very long ranges they can be intercepted and DF'd over similar distances and the position of a ship or force at sea compromised. ELOS frequencies are not so dangerous, since they are chosen to carry over the required range and attenuate rapidly beyond this. However, nature is not always cooperative, and they can on occasions travel over much longer distances. The need to control radio and electronic emissions in a task force, as part of the tactical command process, was discussed in Chapter 3.

Communications Security is a particular term used to describe a communication system's ability to withstand enemy crypto-analytical attack. Put another way, it is a measure of the protection afforded to communications traffic by its cryptographic systems. Nowadays, crypto-systems are, almost without exception, machine based; the days of manual cyphers are virtually over. Crypto-systems can be off-line, which protect individual messages, or on-line, which protect the data stream transmitted over a circuit. The latter is greatly superior as the enemy intercept service is unable to follow what is going on since transmission is indecipherable. Most teleprinter and data communications circuits are crypto-protected by on-line machine systems; many voice circuits are similarly covered by 'speech secrecy' equipment, particularly those carrying high-level conference traffic. Such insecurity that remains is therefore caused principally by use of voice circuits that are not yet crypto-covered.

Speed

Speed of communication during naval operations is highly desirable, and sometimes essential—for instance, manoeuvring signals which require precise execution. However Reliability, Security and Speed tend to pull against one another, and the first two must normally take priority. In cases where speed is essential it must be accepted that reliability or security may be sacrificed. This is so with enemy reports, which are one of the occasions when HF silence may be broken without prior authority.

Delays may occur in two ways. A message may have to wait its turn with others for transmission over a circuit; and in the case of messages passed over a network, delays may also be incurred whilst they wait in sorting piles for onward routing. Force communications are prone to circuit delays, particularly in the case of voice nets with many stations participating. Waiting one's turn to transmit can be serious if the information is urgent. Such nets may become clogged with voice traffic in a busy operational situation. Good circuit discipline will improve matters, but in general the fewer ships or aircraft on the net the better. There may, however, be insufficient radio equipment to make the ideal circuit organisation possible.

Written messages frequently require routing over extensive networks, and suffer both types of delay. The effect is mitigated by the Precedence system, described above. Messages will be normally Routine, but urgent administrative signals may be afforded Priority, whilst urgent operational traffic may be given either Priority or Immediate; Flash may be used only on short and vital types of signal such as enemy reports. At each stage of transmission or sorting, messages are handled in order of precedence. The precedence system will therefore usually result in the higher categories getting through in good time, but backlogs of lower precedence messages can build up. In such circumstances it may be necessary to order 'MINIMISE', a general instruction to originators to reduce signalling to the essential minimum needed to support operations. The problem is not confined to naval communications—in fact it affects all military communications. It applies particularly to NATO, where the elaborate command structure and the propensity of originators to include too many authorities in a message address tends to proliferate not only the number of messages but also the number of transmissions per message. The advent of satellite communications, with their high traffic capacity, and the introduction of computerised routing and switching equipment, has improved the situation. There is, nevertheless, a reverse side to this coin; the success of the communications system in delivering an increasing flood of message traffic on time means that operational staffs may now be overwhelmed by the sheer volume of information to be digested. One answer to this problem is the introduction of CCIS—command, control and information systems—which provide a degree of pre-digestion in the form of computerised sorting and presentation of message traffic. Such systems are discussed more fully in the next chapter.

6

Command and Computers

IN the previous four chapters we have seen how sensors provide tactical information, and how radio communications allow information and orders to be exchanged between naval units and their commanders. This information gathering and dissemination represents a prodigious flow, which has to be digested, analysed, and acted upon. In the past, this command and control process was handled as a manual operation—signals were in hard copy form, information on each aspect of an operation was held in ops rooms in neat clips, tactical information was displayed and updated on manual plots, decisions were reached by personal discussion between commanders and their staffs, and the resulting signals were originated in writing. This was adequate when reactions to threats could be measured in minutes, which applied to warfare in which sub-sonic aircraft attacked with bombs, conventionally powered submarines attacked with torpedoes, and a ship's principal surface weapon was the gun. Over the last decade or so all this has changed—steadily but dramatically. The shell, the bomb and the torpedo have been replaced by the supersonic missile as the principal weapon of attack; sea skimming delivery has reduced warning time to seconds; guidance techniques have led to stand-off tactics; and satellite surveillance has exposed the oceans to the gaze of the enemy. The situation confronting the force commander and his captains at sea today is a world apart from that facing their counterparts of twenty or thirty years ago. It is not surprising that the way they command and fight their ships is also quite different. In this chapter we shall see how the information available is presented to them by computers and used to solve their tactical problems, rapidly and reliably.

The process of change began with the advent of radar in World War II. This led to the introduction in the Royal Navy of the Action Information Organisation (AIO), with manual plots and remote control of the ships' radio communications situated in the Operations Room. (The American term is Combat Information Center or CIC.) Here the captain and admiral would conduct affairs when action was about to be joined. Hitherto, command of a ship or force in action had been conducted from the bridge, from where the ship was navigated and which gave the best view of the situation. Radar showed that when fighting, rather than navigation, was the concern of the command, the commander had to move to where radar and the associated tactical plots were displayed. The next step occurred during the 1950s, as the speed of warfare increased with aircraft delivered missiles becoming a prime threat to surface ships. It became apparent that for the captain to move to the Operations Room when action was imminent was inadequate; warning times were being reduced, and he could arrive too late to take charge of the rapidly developing situation. The NATO navies gradually recognised that in war the primary position for the captain and the admiral was the Operations Room, and that they needed deputies who could act for them when they were resting. The bridge remained the place from where the ship was conned in close quarters situations like replenishment at sea, whilst berthing, and in cruising conditions, but in defence conditions it required only an experienced officer as a 'ship safety' expert.

However, not all navies moved at the same time to this almost sacrilegious abandonment of the bridge; in particular the USN continued to believe for several years that the captain's proper place was where he could best exercise his paramount responsibility for the safety of his ship and that the fighting of the ship could be deputed to his Operations Officer. During the period that contrary philosophies were in force an unsuspected problem was encountered. Tactical radio nets are operated at positions where the information they carry is required and generated. Those navies which had moved the command position to the Ops Room increasingly used radio nets terminated there to carry messages of command significance. However, if the force included ships whose captains were still on the bridge, they might remain unaware of what had been passed; moreover a message originated in the operations room from such a ship would lack the captain's personal authority. It might appear surprising that such a seemingly simple matter could cause difficulty, but in the heat of action, when seconds are vital, the nuances of communications must be correctly understood by those in command, or serious misunderstandings can occur. The problem lasted only a few years during the transitional period, but it illustrates a wider point: where and how men interact with the equipment they operate (the man/machine interface) is just as vital a system feature as more material characteristics.

During the 1960s and 1970s, both the USN and the RN introduced a new sort of equipment, the tactical automatic data processor, or tactical computer. The American system was the Naval Tactical Data System (NTDS), and the compatible RN system was named Action Data Automation (ADA). Another new element, a tactical form of digital data link, known as Link 11, was introduced simultaneously as part of the system. These revolutionary systems were installed in carriers and their supporting guided missile ships, and were aimed at automating the air defence of the fleet. By this time, air defence was presenting problems of both scale and response, solutions to which were beyond the scope of manual methods. However, the new tactical computer systems not only changed naval air defence, they also ushered in the command and control revolution. The facilities they provided for senior officers were far in advance of anything previously available and captains discovered that they had the choice of either operating their own computer consoles in the ops room and keeping in constant touch with the situation, or remaining in isolation on the bridge. The early versions of NTDS and ADA were too large, and also too expensive, to be fitted in smaller warships like frigates. In the Royal Navy, which was coming to terms with becoming a largely frigate force, this was unwelcome, and a smaller semi-automatic system, CAAIS (Computer Assisted Action Information System) was introduced. This also needed a smaller capacity data link, known as Link 10. These systems were stop-gaps however. As soon as computer technology could provide fully automatic systems at an acceptable size and cost, all major warships in the RN were fitted with them and Link 11 became the standard naval data link. Nowadays, every modern navy has tactical ADP at the heart of its command system. We shall now look at the main operational features of such systems in greater detail.

Tactical Computer Systems

Terminology can be confusing. A 'command system' (an ambiguous term if taken literally) is often used to refer to a tactical computer system which serves the command and control process. A better term is being introduced, the Combat Direction System or CDS, the name given to the collection of computers which, when organised as a system, provide all the facilities for directing the fighting capabilities of a warship. This includes the ability for command and control, but also covers the semi-autonomous computer sub-systems which control each sensor and weapon. The term Command System is sometimes used to refer to that part of the CDS which serves the command and control function. We will examine the main characteristics of a modern CDS, since this illustrates the degree to which computerised control is now used to direct modern naval warfare, the facilities offered to the command for the purpose and the implications for command and control stemming from this new technology.

Every CDS will be tailor-made for its class of ship and the type of weapons fitted; a typical system is illustrated schematically in Figure 6.1, a highly simplified example to illustrate the main features. Weapons and sensors will have data processors to provide their own digital control, and sensors will execute a degree of pre-procesing of their information (eg to remove clutter, resolve target ambiguities, and arrange the information in suitable form for further processing) before it is passed to the central processor for correlation, analysis and track generation. The function of interconnecting several subordinate sensors and weapon systems involves considerable organisation and control, independent of the central picture processing, and this function will probably be performed by a separate computer sub-system known as the data bus controller. Sensor information reaching the central processor will, of course, be in real time, but much other information available to the central computer will be of a semi-permanent nature, sometimes known as status information. This includes such facts as own ship's weapons characteristics and ammunition state and semi-permanent information on the capabilities of ships of the force. In addition, a status tote will be kept of the availability of weapons and aircraft of ships in company, passed and up-dated via data links. All this semi-permanent information is stored centrally in the main data store, together with the computer program which controls and drives the whole system. Human control over the system is effected from the system controller's console; generally speaking this is limited to switching on and off, selection of system mode and user checks on performance.

FIGURE 6.1

CENTRALISED COMBAT DIRECTION SYSTEM

Schematic Diagram

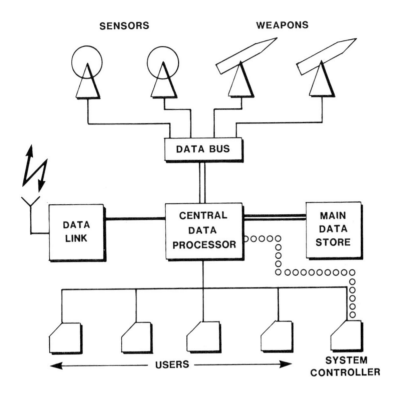

Human use of the CDS is effected from the tactical display consoles, of which there may be 10 to 20 in a major warship. Every officer or senior rating who forms part of the command and control team must either have access to such an equipment or effectively be excluded. Plate 6.1 shows the facilities at such a console. There are two video display units (VDUs), one showing the tactical picture as a two-dimensional positional display, and the other an alpha-numeric display giving information on specific tracks, status information on requested subjects, menu information allowing choice of mode and data and answers to queries and tactical problems. Control is provided by means of a keyboard—very similar to that on a personal computer—and a rolling ball (similar to a 'mouse') to operate a cursor which is used to point to items of interest. Information on a track is obtained by placing the cursor on it and then keying in the instruction to display the required category. The facilities at the console are completed by providing each user with microphone and earphones; channel selectors allow him to communicate internally with others in his team, and (for those with the need to do so) externally on appropriate voice nets.

It is therefore no longer necessary—indeed inappropriate—for officers to

PLATE 6.1   A typical modern tactical display console. (*Courtesy Racal Electronics*)

cluster around a manual plot to discuss the situation and decide future action. If the captain wishes to draw the attention of one of his officers to a track he will call him on his intercom (probably, as captain, with a break-in facility) place his cursor over the track with his rolling ball, and pose his question. The officer may reply verbally, or alternatively may call up the relevant track information on the alpha-numeric screens, so that both officers can discuss this in detail. Changing to this way of conducting command and control was a revolutionary step for many senior officers. It requires a good understanding of the equipment and its potentialities and the whole ship's team must be trained together. Command team training is a vital part of a ship's work up before deploying for operational service, and is done in the Royal Navy onshore, using highly sophisticated computerised trainers at the School of Maritime Operations at HMS *Dryad* outside Portsmouth. Subsequent training and exercises to maintain efficiency can be done on board, using the computers in training modes of operation, and in exercises at sea with other ships. Increasingly, nowadays, tactical computer systems use colour video displays. Colour is used to distinguish between different types of information, for instance hostile tracks may be in red, friendly in green, neutral in yellow, and new or urgent threats in white. The associated totes would be in similar colours. This adds clarity to the picture and highlights important details, thus allowing users to concentrate on information most relevant to their tasks. This is important, as anything which reduces the strain of looking at video displays for long periods lowers the demands on the individual and increases efficiency.

The tactical picture is available to each user on call up at each console. This basic function is supplemented, again on request by the user, by solutions to tactical problems, such as correct courses to steer for rendezvous and collision avoidance, vector analysis of aircraft interceptions, and, most importantly, evaluation of the threats facing the force and the available options to counter them. Activity on the part of the computer is therefore partly automatic and partly on demand. For example, all tracks which are classified as hostile will be treated without further instruction as threats, and the degree to which they threaten the force assessed by reference to their course and speed and likely weapons. Tracks classified as unknown may be treated as hostile if their behaviour is threatening (for example an aircraft closing the force at high speed). Tracks with an unknown identity will be watched to see if their behaviour or other information on them necessitates a change in status. However, any track which is assessed by one of the control officers may be re-categorised as a result of his judgement; he would do this by placing his cursor on the track and entering the appropriate information into the tote. As a result of all this activity the picture will be far more meaningful than that which would be obtained from radar alone. Every track will have an indication as to whether it is friendly, neutral, hostile or unknown and all information on it will be available on the

PLATE 6.2   The Ferranti Integrated Submarine Command System (FISCS). (*Courtesy Ferranti*)

associated tote. Tracks which pose particularly dangerous threats may have additional tags associated with them, such as winking lights or audio alarms.

The amount of information held in the computer stores would be bewildering if it were all displayed together. What is displayed on each screen is what its user needs. The aircraft direction officer will need air tracks, the electronic warfare officer will need ESM detections and bearing lines. Each user can further subdivide what is shown by use of his 'category selection' controls. This is particularly useful to the captain or his deputy, who in the height of battle are probably not directly interested in exactly how the direction officer is controlling a fighter to intercept an incoming attacker, provided he is dealing with that threat. Of more interest to the command at this point will be to know that all threats are being countered, and that no unknown tracks which might prove hostile are getting into dangerous positions. The captain can therefore select for display on his VDU all hostiles and all unknowns. From his tote he can see which friendly aircraft are engaging which hostile aircraft and which ships are engaging incoming raids with missiles. This should give him a good picture of the overall threat and the extent to which it is being dealt with. The ability to access the critical information needed from the large common data base is one of the most valuable features of tactical computer systems.

Automatic Weapon Response

The process of threat evaluation and weapon allocation is known as TEWA. Weapon allocation is an especially valuable facility provided by the tactical computer, since it explores in rigorous detail every possible response, queues them in a calculated order of advantage, answers queries on the implications of each choice and, when a decision is made, takes the necessary action to initiate weapon use. If this process were attempted using manual methods it would take many minutes and still probably suffer from lack of completeness; with the computer it will take only seconds, and most of this will be the time spent in human consideration and judgement. An extension of this procedure may be used to combat under automatic control really urgent threats. In modern naval warfare some offensive weapons may be detected by the defence only seconds before they hit. The sea skimming missile (such as the French EXOCET or the British SEA EAGLE) are potent examples. Launched from long range under inertial guidance and transmitting at a height of only a few metres, it will be detected by the defence at a range of about 5–10 kilometres at best. With its near-sonic speed of approach it will impact with the target 20 seconds or so later. Any counter-measure, for example an anti-missile missile such as SEA WOLF, must be launched within seconds. Accelerating to supersonic speed, it will intercept and destroy the attacking missile at a distance from the ship of, say, two kilometres or less. A margin of safety hardly exists, and the plain fact is that there is no time for human consideration and judgement. Launching of the defensive weapon must occur virtually simultaneously with identification of the incoming threat.

Rapid weapons response of the type that is clearly needed in modern warfare can, in fact, be accomplished with the sort of modern sensors described in previous chapters, integrated with tactical computer systems under discussion. The rules governing identification of the threat can be written very narrowly and precisely and the computer programmed to initiate launching of the defensive anti-missile missile against its target without further instructions. It will of course be possible and appropriate to design the system so that the human command can over-ride the action, by using the system controls to abort the launch during the few seconds before the missile is actually away, or to destroy it in flight. Use of automatic response in this manner should not be viewed as surrendering responsibility to the computer. The action is analogous to the cocking of a gun which will fire on being triggered by a trip wire, a deliberate human act which would be taken only in appropriate circumstances and after due warnings.

The responsibilities and functions of the Command in relation to such automatic response lie in two fields. First, as a continuing action beforehand, to ensure that the rules contained in the software which classify a target as an urgent menace (ie the trigger) are valid and are kept updated as necessary. Second, during operations to decide the degree to which such weapons are to be allowed freedom to fire automatically, and thus to order the appropriate weapon control mode. This positive action would only occur after shipping and aircraft in the region had been warned, probably backed by the declaration of zones of exclusion. Moreover, the use of weapons in this way would be subject to the same degree of control as all naval activity in periods of confrontation, namely the politically authorised 'Rules of Engagement', discussed in the next chapter.

The use of such automatic weapon response is a most significant step in naval tactics. It is also an interesting example of military science at work. The requirement was generated by the need to combat a novel and dangerous threat, anti-ship missiles, created by one branch of defence technology, namely aerodynamics. The solution, computer control of sensors and weapons, came from another branch, information technology. The procedures for bringing this potent extension of naval capability under an appropriate degree of command and control were developed in parallel. We have used the case of an attack by sea skimming missiles, countered by anti-missile missiles, to illustrate this discussion. However, the technique can, of course, be used far more widely; for example, exactly similar techniques can be used to control Close In Weapons Systems (CIWS) like VULCAN/PHALANX or GOALKEEPER to combat low flying aircraft. We are likely to see the extension of such automatic modes of warfare in future years, as weapon delivery speeds increase and reaction times reduce.

Distributed Computer Systems

In fact, the demand for such rapid response taxes even a computer's ability, and the need to react within a few seconds can pose an impossible task in a busy situation with several threats occurring simultaneously. The centralised architecture of the computer systems discussed above represents a contributory cause to this problem. In Figure 6.1 it will be seen that all actions have to pass through the central processor. Despite the power and speed of modern computers, this inevitably means queuing, and thus delays, during busy conditions. The solution is one which is already available from modern technology and in fact is already being implemented for different reasons. The advent of small computers is rapidly leading to systems in which the processing function is no longer fully centralised in one big computer, but dispersed amongst several smaller ones. Such a system is known as a distributed system; Figure 6.2 illustrates the principles. Notice that all the components of the centralised system of Figure 6.1 are retained, but organised differently. Each component has its own processing unit and all are interconnected via the data highway (sometimes called a local area network) with its own control processor. The main functional difference, apart from the different structure (or system architecture as it is termed), is that much of the processing which in the first version was carried out in the central

FIGURE 6.2

DISTRIBUTED COMBAT DIRECTION SYSTEM

Schematic Diagram

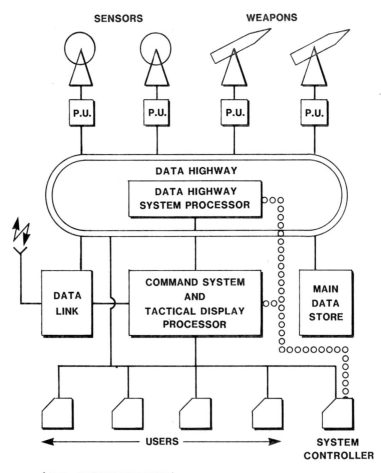

(P.U. PROCESSOR UNIT)

processor, is now performed in the sub-systems. An example will illustrate this: the recognition on the part of a sensor—say an ESM equipment—that a detected track must be engaged under automatic response is carried out in the ESM processor. The data message initiating the response is addressed to the appropriate weapon, and is recognised by the system control processor and routed direct to the weapon for action. In parallel, the data message is also routed to the command system processor, where it is added to the tactical data and displayed on the tactical consoles. This parallel action enables a much faster reaction.

The rapid response of a distributed system is an important advantage, but in fact there are wider arguments in favour of such architecture. The advent of the micro-processor has made it unnecessary to use expensive 'number crunching' computers to provide the overall system power needed, provided the necessary number of smaller processors can be organised into effective systems. This is not only cheaper but more efficient. As we have seen, for some important functions it is faster. It also allows a greater degree of reliability to be designed into the system. One of the problems of the centralised system is its proneness to catastrophic failure—the 'single bullet syndrome'. By contrast, the dispersed nature of the architecture of the distributed system means that malfunction of one component does not mean complete system failure, particularly if the data highway has a measure of 'self healing'. The reconfiguration of remaining components into a planned fallback mode of system operation may well enable the system to operate with only minor loss of overall efficiency; such a progression is sometimes known as 'graceful degradation'. Furthermore, as components in a distributed system are individually a good deal cheaper than the equivalent major elements in a centralised system it is practicable to duplicate vital parts of the system, thus providing a degree of redundancy and automatic damage resistance. A further advantage of a distributed system is that it is relatively easier to up-date parts of it by sub-system replacement, thus extending useful service life. All in all, the move to distributed architectures for tactical computer systems is a significant development, and most tactical computer systems are now being designed in this way. It must, however, be said that distributed computer systems create their own internal problems, as they need to be designed and created in accordance with a strict architecture and rigorously applied technical standards if all components are to interoperate successfully. This is another example of the more general problem of interoperability, discussed in the previous chapter.

Data Links

So far the system that we have been describing is internal to one ship. However the potential of computers for tactical command and control is only realised to the full if all ships of the force (and where appropriate their cooperating aircraft) can be linked automatically to exchange data between computers. This permits the sensors of all ships to be utilised to provide a wider and more comprehensive picture than that obtainable from one ship alone, and all weapons available in the force can be coordinated to provide the most economical and effective response. The facility which provides this capability is known as a data link.

In concept the data link is a simple device. It takes an organised stream of information from its parent computer and causes it to be transmitted to other ships of the force. In turn, it receives similar information from other ships of the force and passes this into its parent computer. In practice, however, the design and operation of a practicable system is a highly complex matter. A data link is characterised by three different sets of features: first the stream of information which has to be exchanged; second the technical details of the electronics equipment which enable the information stream to be transmitted and received by radio; and third the procedures and conventions which govern the operation of data exchange and the use of the information. Let us look at each of these in turn.

Computers operate with the binary code (0s and 1s) and any communication between them must do so too. A stream of 0s and 1s—known as 'bits', short for binary digits—is meaningless unless its coding is understood by each end of the system, which means that it must transcend the programming of each computer (which will, of course, vary from ship to ship). Data link information is therefore transmitted in formatted messages, known as message standards, which are devised and agreed internationally. There is a strong analogy with the International Code of Signals, which establishes coded messages which transcend national language.

The bit stream generated by the computer is used to control the transmitter via an equipment known as a 'modem' (short for modulator/demodulator). This converts the bits into audio signals which are then used to modulate a suitable radio transmitter. Modulation allows an HF transmitter to carry information at a much higher data rate (typically 2400 bits/seconds) than, for instance, that required for teleprinter traffic. If UHF transmission is used then audio modulation may be dispensed with and an equivalent result achieved by high-speed direct keying. In the receiving ship, the radio signal is passed back into the modem, where the reverse process is carried out, known as demodulation. This regenerates the bit stream in the form suitable for the computer, to which it is then passed. The process is usually accompanied by encryption of the data stream before transmission, by encoding it with a high-grade on-line crypto key, with the reverse occurring on reception. Figure 6.3 is a simplified schematic diagram showing the basic components of a data link system.

To make a data link work in practice requires strict procedures to be followed, known as the link protocols. Space does not permit the whole subject to be discussed but an example will illustrate the point. As regards the transmission sequence, there can be no human intervention once the data link is operating. There are two common automatic methods: the simpler is known as Time Slot, in which each computer is allocated a number of seconds of transmission time during a cycle of established length. For example, with six ships participating, each might be allocated two seconds in a cycle of twelve seconds. This is a typical cycle time which will produce an up-date from each ship at twelve-second intervals, yet still allow a large number of messages to be passed in each slot. Time slot procedure is easy to operate; the start time is synchronised accurately and each computer transmits during its allotted period. It is however inflexible and potentially inefficient, since the time needed by each ship to report its contacts, will vary as the situation develops. A more responsive method is known as 'Round Robin', in which the sequence of transmission is fixed, but each ship transmits for as long as is necessary to clear all outstanding messages. The last message to be transmitted will include a code indicating there is no more to come. This triggers the next ship to begin.

Greater problems are generated by the procedure for use of the information. When information is exchanged between humans via radio net, queries and corrections can be resolved by the application of professional judgement and common sense. Computers have neither of these qualities, other than the actions they have been programmed to obey. In the early days of data links it was discovered that an astonishing degree of detail had to be written into the protocols if smooth operation, particularly between ships of different nations, was to be achieved. Again, one example will illustrate the point. If several ships hold a track on their radars, they will all report it (which is inefficient use of the data link) unless only one is selected to do so. The rules for deciding which ship should report must be agreed and written into the link protocols so that all computers conform. A measure of the track quality of each ship's echo must be devised to allow a simple choice to be made, and a bidding procedure must be followed to decide which ship continues to report.

The data link extends the picture compiled by the tactical computer from a

FIGURE 6.3

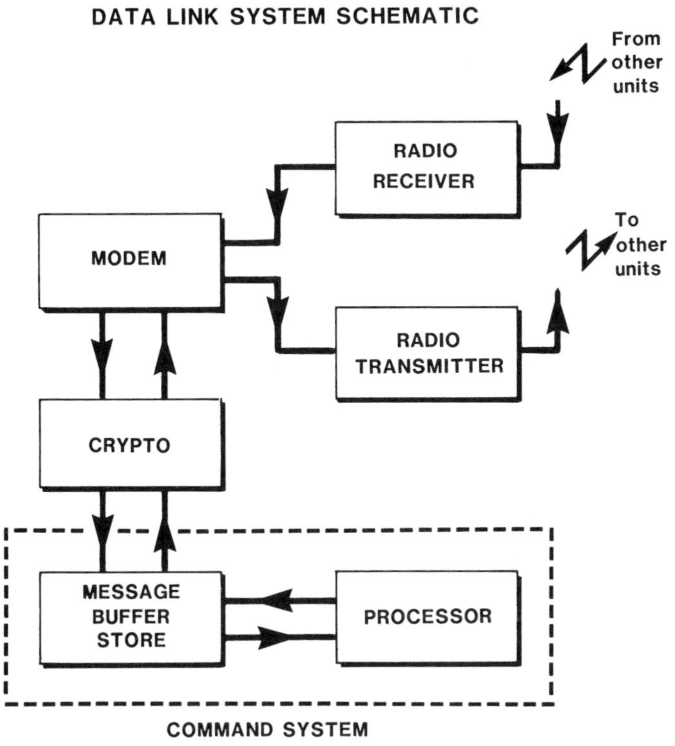

DATA LINK SYSTEM SCHEMATIC

COMMAND SYSTEM

purely internal one relying on own ships sensors, to an external one involving other ships and aircraft. This creates one of the more intractable problems to be met in applying information technology to naval requirements, namely the need for accurate platform position. The reader is referred to the section dealing with radio navigation and radio positioning systems in Chapter 2, which describes this problem and how it is being tackled. To summarise, unless a ship's position relative to other platforms is known very accurately, it is impossible to link up (ie correlate) its radar reports with those from such other ships and aircraft. If high positional accuracy is not available, reported tracks will be represented in the computer store by moving 'points' which should, in practice, be more correctly plotted as moving 'areas' in order to allow for the positional uncertainty. A target reported by data link may therefore generate a number of separate tracks, one for each platform reporting it, since the computer will be unable to recognise them as originating from the same source. Although a human being could resolve this situation, to decide how best to show one track only by applying common-sense, this is beyond a computer. Unless corrected, the situation would lead to unacceptable degradation of the tactical picture. The long-term solution is to provide sufficiently accurate positional information to all platforms, and this underlines the importance of the Global Positioning System (GPS) due to be introduced during the next few years. Pending its introduction, however, the only solution is to provide a degree of human supervision; a separate voice net links all data link participants for general control of the link. Amongst other things, this is used for the coordination of Track Management, as the subject is termed.

A number of data links have been established for use within NATO. Of these the most widely fitted is Link 11, the fully automatic tactical link, installed not only in most major warships of the Alliance but also in many maritime patrol and reconnaissance aircraft, and Air Warning and Control System (AWACS) aircraft. Link 11 also interconnects with its counterpart ashore, Link 1, via a computer system known as a 'buffer', which automatically arranges for the exchange of data between the two links. The buffer reorganises both information streams to make them compatible with recipient systems. This is helped by the fact that their message standards are identical in many respects; however the positional problems outlined in the previous paragraph bedevil the process, because the Link 1 standards, being designed for static use, carry no such information, and the buffer must insert its own artificial position. Link 14 is an important facility in a NATO force; it is a man-readable, computer-generated teleprinter broadcast, which enables non-computer-fitted ships to plot manually, or semi-automatically, a summary of the most important information available to better equipped ships. We should also note the likely advent of Link 16 during the 1990s, with its counterpart equipment JTIDS. The advantages of this new type of information distribution system were discussed in the previous chapter.

Command, Control and Information Systems (CCIS)

The magnitude of the command and control task facing senior naval officers and their staffs has led to the introduction of widespread shore-based, computer-based systems. The nature of the problem has its parallels with that in ships, but there are important differences. In a task force, the principal need, as we have seen, is to assimilate and analyse tactical information on the local environment in time to initiate effective action against a very fast moving enemy. This means that tactical computers must be real time systems, capable of absorbing and reacting to the flow of information in step with events as they occur. Ashore there is not this paramount urgency; decisions will be required within minutes, but not normally within seconds. The problem in shore headquarters is to receive, correlate and present the huge amount of information available from the long-range intelligence systems we have been studying, and to absorb and react to the vast flow of information reaching commanders and their staffs via modern communications systems. This having been done, there is a further need to coordinate the resulting action between naval commanders world wide, remembering the need for close control in times of tension. Computer-based systems to meet these requirements can be considered under two heads—the information handling systems in shore headquarters, and the satellite communications data networks linking commanders and their headquarters.

Most senior naval officers commanding sea areas now have CCIS systems installed in their headquarters. The facilities at the Maritime Headquarters, Northwood, Middlesex, in England, is an example. This is the combined headquarters of the Royal Navy's Commander-in-Chief, Fleet, and also NATO's Allied Commander-in-Chief, Channel, and Commander-in-Chief,

PLATE 6.3   Northwood Maritime HQ. General view of the Operations Room showing the user consoles and other facilities associated with the OPCON CCIS. (*Courtesy NAVAL FORCES. Crown Copyright/RN photograph*)

Eastern Atlantic. All three posts are held by one officer 'wearing three hats' as described in Chapter 1, with separate British and NATO staffs serving him in the discharge of his respective national and international responsibilities. In the underground headquarters there are two sets of operations rooms and supporting cells. The CCIS system is known as 'OPCON' and it has enabled the operational control of national and allied forces under the operational command of the Commander-in-Chief, other than those assigned to subordinate commanders, to be centralised under the C-in-C. Hitherto only operational command (a rather remote function) was exercised from Northwood, all ships being assigned to the operational control of subordinate commanders for their detailed direction.

The facilities available from OPCON are amongst the best of their type in the world. They are shared between national and NATO staffs on a similar basis and we will not distinguish between them. The heart of the system is its ability to absorb, correlate and display information on a wide variety of subjects, from ships' positions and movements to the capabilities of weapons. Incoming information is received from conventional communications and digital networks, the latter discussed below. As far as possible all communication to Northwood is formatted in accordance with ADatP3, as explained in Chapter 5. This enables it to be injected automatically into the system stores, where it is correlated by subject matter. The process is supervised by human operators who confirm and, if necessary, correct the computer's decisions, and also arrange for any unformatted messages to be handled by humans for analysis and injection. If an incoming report is urgent, it will be brought to the immediate attention of a duty officer, but if it adds to existing knowledge of the subject it will be stored in its subject file and the relevant status display will carry an indication that there is new information available. Users access the information they need from VDU consoles very similar to those in ships, with geographical and tote displays, cursors and keyboards.

Incoming signals are presented by VDU with follow-up hard copy if required; outgoing signals can be drafted on the VDU, shown to other positions by VDU and discussed by intercom, and when approved for origination passed automatically to the communications office for transmission, already in digital format. In addition to information and intelligence on the developing operational situation, an enormous amount of semi-permanent data is available on demand, such as the weapon characteristics of every ship in the Royal Navy, or the current maintenance state of HMS *Nonsuch*'s Type ABC radar. It is not difficult to see that such systems have revolutionised how fleets are controlled from ashore.

Satellite Command Networks

Further application of computer and satellite technology has been made by the United States to provide global command and control systems. The most extensive of these is the World Wide Military Command and Control System (WWMCCS). As its name implies, this system is not purely naval or maritime, but provides a means for the high level direction of all the armed forces. Its scale is well beyond the compass of other NATO nations, but the WWMCCS interoperates with European and NATO headquarters by integrating them, with appropriate segregation of national and allied channels, into the associated data networks, mainly provided by satellite. The heart of WWMCCS is its enormous information base, which is continually being updated from the theatre-wide surveillance systems described elsewhere in this book. The collection and processing of this information requires very extensive resources: satellites and their payloads; radio listening stations; ocean bed installations and underwater cables; long-range data networks and banks of computers and digital storage bureaux. The intelligence is comprehensively catalogued and correlated so that all data on one contact or event is brought together and made available for evaluation and strategic use. It is complemented by information on friendly and allied movements and status reports.

Moving all this information around is a major task in itself, requiring to be separately organised and controlled; this is done by using a subordinate digital data transmission network, under semi-autonomous control; other inter-computer digital systems associated with WWMCCS are also separately organised, so, in effect, WWMCCS is a vast 'system of systems'. The resulting data base and network structure forms both the information source for compiling and presenting the current and forecast situation and for inter-command communication and direction. WWMCCS thus informs and links commanders from the highest political level down to area commander. All connected headquarters are equipped in similar fashion to Northwood. Seagoing commanders with appropriately equipped flagships are also included in the system, linked by satellite as effectively as if they were situated ashore. The result is a web of command which is not only interactively linked for decision making but which has access to a common data base. The importance of the latter point is often overlooked; if commanders are taking decisions on differing information and intelligence, the opportunity for misunderstanding and false judgements is greatly increased.

Hardware and Software

This chapter has described how information technology has been applied to naval command and control, and tactics; these developments represent one of the greatest changes that navies have faced in the manner of how naval resources are deployed and operated. Moreover, the revolution goes wider: the Royal Navy's latest frigate, the Type 23, has no fewer than 220 data processors onboard (48 for the command system, 40 for communications, 50 for weapons/sensors systems, 41 for weapons control, 35 for marine machinery control and 6 for administration and logistics). We have examined the reasons for such rapid and widespread growth of computers, which can be summarised thus:

> The volume of information available from modern sensors is beyond the capacity of humans to analyse and digest without the processing power of computers.
> The reaction times resulting from the speed of modern warfare necessitate decisions being reached in seconds. This needs at least some assistance from computers, and in many cases requires carefully regulated automatic response.
> Computers can optimise the use of machines in accordance with carefully calculated procedures and control sequences, and supervise such operation accurately and indefinitely, without the limitation of human endurance.

For applications where the use of computers is valid, it is possible to reduce personnel, and probably increase both capability and efficiency and save operating costs.

However, such extensive use of computers carries with it a most important corollary. Computers do not run themselves, they are under the control of programs and other forms of instruction, the generic term for which is software. Software is the mind which drives the body. The success of an automatic engagement which results in the countering of an enemy attack is just as dependent on the correct writing of the software as the correct design and functioning of the hardware—the computers, the radars, and the missiles. The writing, checking and updating of software is therefore a critically important function, on which a wide variety of naval activity increasingly depends.

Software starts life in the laboratory, and is an essential part of system design. Indeed many computer-based systems are founded on their software, the hardware being designed around it. In the military field, where state of the art technology is essential, the mathematics behind advanced software will probably represent the frontiers of human understanding. At the time of writing this book, such subjects as linear predictive coding, pattern recognition, adaptive processing, and de-interleaving algorithms are examples of where research is looking. What is certain is that in a few years time these subjects will have been supplanted by new ones. At its heart, therefore, software is a highly esoteric subject. The problem for the command, which will eventually have to use it and rely on it, is how to ensure that, when it reaches the Fleet, it works effectively. At this stage one must recognise that the term 'command' necessarily encompasses two levels. The design and engineering of new systems, including their software, is the responsibility of higher command, in this case the Ministry of Defence, working in conjunction with its own research establishments and industry. Later, when the result reaches the Fleet, admirals and captains will be concerned to understand how their system software works, what operational procedures they and their staffs must follow to use it correctly and, most importantly, that it provides and continues to provide the required reaction and performance.

The concern of command with software can therefore be said to occur at three stages of a system's life. At the inception stage, it is to ensure that it accurately addresses the operational requirement. Second, at the stage of introduction into service, it is to ensure that it works correctly (ie is 'debugged' before being turned over to ships' staffs). Finally, during its operational life, to use it correctly and keep it up-dated as the threat and other factors change. We have likened software to a computer's mind; it is the function of command, by controlling its software, to provide its soul.

7

Command and Control of Naval Operations

THE earlier chapters have described the main elements of naval command and control, its organisation and structure, the sources of information, the means of processing it and the techniques of naval communications. Let us now see how these constituents are brought together for the direction of naval operations.

Surface warships still provide the main strength of a modern navy, despite the importance of submarines and aircraft in naval warfare, and it is not difficult to see why. The location and clearance of mines, the protection of merchant shipping, the policing of fishing grounds and offshore oil rigs and the deployment of carrier-based air power beyond the range of shore-based aircraft: these and similar operations would be beyond the capacity of a navy comprised principally of submarines with shore-based air support. As we shall see later, the command and control of naval and maritime aircraft, of amphibious operations and of submarine operations, require their own special measures, but the basic organisation of naval command and control is built on the need to direct the activities of the surface fleet.

Warships being specialised vessels, most naval operations involve numbers of ships acting together, to provide a force with the required balance of capabilities. Today's naval task force is the equivalent of the battlefleet of history, and the coordination and direction of its varied and far-flung components is a demanding function which constitutes a major element of the command and control process. Warships also operate alone, for example on passage, when acting as a guard-ship, or on rescue missions. And naval forces, of whatever size or composition, can be deployed inshore or in deep ocean, in home waters or on the other side of the world. Such variety in the pattern of operations calls for a system for their command and control of long reach and wide versatility. It must also be hierarchical in nature, operating at many levels and providing the authoritative overlay for virtually all naval activity.

At the highest level (ie political) the defence ministry will in times of tension be concerned primarily to deter aggression and avoid war. This could involve a period of rising tension in which opposing forces were deployed in confrontation without direct military action occurring. This would be a situation of great danger, in which false moves could be misinterpreted, leading to the unintentional outbreak of hostilities. The need for tight control in such a scenario is self-evident: dependable information, reliable communications, rapid analysis and

111

PLATE 7.1   Egyptian patrol vessel of the RAMADAN Class undergoing sea trials. The increasing importance of an off-shore naval capability has led many navies to order small but well armed craft of similar type. (*Courtesy Vosper Thornycroft*)

thoroughly understood command procedures would be vital. In such situations, a special set of instructions to operational and tactical commanders would be used, known as 'Rules of Engagement'. These are sets of comprehensive orders on how ships and aircraft are to respond to enemy tactics and the circumstances in which they might use their weapon systems and open fire. Variations within each set can be indicated to suit the situation, so the Rules are very flexible. They are numbered, and the set in force and any variation to it can be ordered by brief signal. The commander-in-chief or supreme commander would be directed by his political authority as to which set was to be effective within the forces under his command. This direction would be changed as the political and operational situation developed. In a war crisis involving NATO, this process would lead to intense international political and diplomatic activity and orders to the Major NATO Commanders would be issued from NATO HQ Brussels.

NATO Operations

Many other activities involving defence ministries and commanders-in-chief would occur during a period of international tension, most of them, in the case of the NATO nations, concerning the military posture of the Alliance. The North Atlantic Treaty is based on the pledge of all signatory nations to act together to

PLATE 7.2   Two Netherlands destroyers attend on an American carrier as plane guards during a NATO exercise. The ability of vessels of different nationality to co-operate closely in such ways is dependent on good communications and common tactical doctrine. (*Courtesy NAVAL FORCES/ Audio Visuele Dienst KM*)

resist aggression committed against any one of them. Most base their defence policies on the assumption that, in the event of aggression on the part of the Warsaw Pact, the resulting military response would be in the form of concerted operations under NATO command rather than individual national action. We have seen in Chapter 1 how the NATO command structure is organised and how national units would be committed to NATO during the Alert Stages of a war crisis. This process of activating national and NATO resources to a state of readiness for operations is known as 'transition to war'. In national capitals, as we have already seen, it would involve government departments putting national activity on a war footing and lead to intense national and international political activity. As far as this book is concerned, we should note that the procedures exist and are exercised regularly in the WINTEX series of command post exercises. Part of the process is the transfer of command of earmarked forces from national to NATO command, most of them at the stage known as Simple Alert.

The ships and supporting aircraft brought together under NATO command will be a mixed force, of many nationalities and with a wide diversity of weapons and other equipment. NATO commanders and their staffs, ashore in their headquarters and supported by their communications facilities, are part of NATO infrastructure and permanently in post. However the 'tactical forces', as ships, aircraft, tanks, field units and so forth, are termed, remain under national command and administration for most of the time in peace. Throughout the history of alliances there have been practical difficulties in creating sufficient cohesion between different national units to provide effective allied fleets and armies. Differences in language, equipment, and tactical doctrine, perhaps accentuated by misplaced national pride, have often led to inefficiency and lack of coordination. It is therefore one of the more remarkable achievements of NATO that it has produced a system in which hastily assembled task forces are immediately effective.

Space does not allow lengthy analysis, but it is of interest to note the main reasons. First, there is a large corpus of written doctrine, the series of Allied Publications, some of which we have already noted in earlier chapters. The most important to naval command and control are the Allied Tactical Publications (ATPs), the Allied Communication Publications (ACPs) and some volumes of the hydrographic and data series (AHPs and ADatPs). These form the basis of common doctrine, which, as we saw in Chapter 1, is essential to command and

PLATE 7.3   The Netherlands destroyer *Pieter Florisz* (while acting as plane guard to a carrier out of picture) is closely marked by the Soviet destroyer *Leningradsky Komsomolets*. During periods of international tension, incidents like this would require very close command and control. (*Courtesy NAVAL FORCES*)

control if voluminous instructions on operational detail are to be avoided. The whole of the series is produced in Washington by an extension of the organisation evolved during World War II, whereby joint committees with supporting staffs drafted and agreed allied plans and procedures. These documents are made available, but not exclusively so, to NATO. They may be offered by the USA, as the custodian, to any defence organisation in what is loosely termed the Western Alliance. This allows them to be used, for example, by the navies of Australia and New Zealand, as partners with the USN and others in the Pacific region pacts. An important point is that most nations which accept them for allied use also use them as their own national publications; this means that the procedures are continuously applied, and become part of normal activity. Thus when ships are 'chopped' (short for change of operational command) to NATO for operations or exercises, they do not have to change the way they behave. If there are national differences, these can be placed in a national annex to the relevant allied publication, rather than produce entirely separate national instructions.

The other reason for NATO's success in creating effective allied naval task forces stems from the realistic exercises that are carried out on a regular basis. These oil the allied machinery for command and control and enable all units of the Alliance to become fully acquainted with NATO procedures and the

PLATE 7.4 Italian warships replenish at sea. The ship-handling skills needed for such close manoeuvres makes a replenishment operation one of the occasions when the Captain would be on the Bridge, to take charge personally. (*Courtesy NAVAL FORCES*)

inevitable slight national differences in naval practice. An important feature of NATO naval operations and exercises is that the only language used for communications is English.

With few exceptions, exercises are the only occasion in peacetime that NATO forces are activated. One of these exceptions is the NATO Airborne Warning and Command Force, which operates NATO owned AWACS aircraft on a continuous basis. The other is the small but politically significant Standing Naval Forces, of which the Standing Naval Force Atlantic (STANAVFORLANT), now 20 years old, is probably the most prominent. This is a mixed force of frigates and vessels of similar size, assigned to NATO command for a period of attachment and so under constant roulement as national units change. The force, which is in near continuous commission, conducts a series of exercises, interspersed by visits to ports in the NATO area. Politically, the existence and evident effectiveness of STANAVFORLANT, and similar standing forces in the Mediterranean and Channel Area, demonstrate NATO's capability and cohesion.

Command and Control of Surface Task Forces

Whether naval operations are conducted under national or NATO command the most frequently used means of organising the ships and aircraft involved will be by the method of Task Organisation described in Chapter 1. This allows a balanced force of units of mixed capabilities to be assembled, disposed and directed with minimum formality. We will now examine the responsibilities at each level of command.

Ashore the main initial concern of defence ministries and commanders-in-chief (in NATO, NATO Headquarters in Brussels and the Major NATO Commanders) would be the resources committed to the operations in progress. We have seen in Chapter 1 how these will have been decided during the planning stage as regards initial deployments. However, as each operation develops, it will be necessary to consider whether further operational or reserve units, or support facilities, are to be committed or whether redeployment from one force to another is called for. An important role of the MOD and its shore-based logistics team is the organisation of the lines of supply and the repair organisation, which remain a national responsibility at all times. This responsibility will be particularly relevant if battle damage has occurred and in the light of ammunition expenditure and requests from the relevant commanders.

At sea, the Task Force Commander must concern himself with the overall progress of the operation and whether this allows him to keep to the intended programme; if not, careful rescheduling will be needed. He must also decide when to order main events, such as force replenishment or an amphibious landing, and if and when to implement changes in the composition of Task Groups in the event of damage or other contingencies. Task Group Commanders will be responsible for ordering the states of readiness of their group, and for disposing their ships to counter enemy threats. They will also be very much concerned with the availability and adequacy of shore-based air support should their groups be operating within range of friendly air bases and will, when necessary, request what they require from the appropriate shore commander. The organisation for command and control of shore-based air support is discussed below.

During operations conducting during a period of tension, there will be special considerations for command at all levels. The posture of opposing forces, in particular their deployments and state of readiness, must be very carefully watched. The need to guard against a possible surprise attack will be very much in the minds of the task force and task group commanders; they will have particular regard to the need to keep the Rules of Engagement amended to allow their ships and aircraft appropriate freedom to respond to hostile acts. This will be a time when the ability to speak direct on secure telephone by satellite, between headquarters ashore and the Task Force Commander, will be especially valuable. At sea, captains and their admirals will be considering the extent to which they can allow their self-defence weapons to respond automatically on warning of missile attack. The EMCON policy in force will require constant review if it imposes any degree of silence, since this will restrict the surveillance cover of the force. And the threat of enemy ECM, a 'soft kill' weapon which might be used in conditions short of overt hostilities, must be borne in mind.

PLATE 7.5   Four vessels of the NATO Standing Naval Force Atlantic (STANAVFORLANT), the Netherlands frigate *De Ruyter* in the foreground. Notice that while each vessel continues to fly its national ensign, all ships of the force also fly the NATO ensign at the starboard yard arm. (*Photo: NATO*)

Many authorities believe that the first stage of modern war is likely to be a period of confusion in which shooting between the armed forces has not yet begun, but during which electronic warfare is used in an attempt to paralyse command and control.

Whatever stage has been reached, ships' captains will be continuously involved with the manoeuvring and states of readiness of their vessels, and with the ordering of weapon response in the event of enemy attack. The need to be able to react instantly to events necessitates their keeping continuously abreast of the situation, absorbing the information from radar and sonar, from intelligence and status reports and from the continuous flow of signals. The concentration required coupled with the responsibility makes command at sea a heavy strain. Moreover, naval operations do not conveniently cease for the night, and combat readiness must be maintained throughout the 24 hours. This makes it essential for admirals and captains to have a system of delegation to their deputies, to allow principals adequate rest and relaxation during operations which may last for weeks. The Admiral will alternate with his Chief of Staff, and the Captain with his Second-in-Command, although they will remain on call at all times for emergencies.

A modern task force may typically number 50 or more vessels, and it will be disposed over a large ocean area. The main elements will probably be deployed within a broad circle of about 100–200 miles radius; inside this tactical area task groups and task units will be operating in closer formations. Single ships will be acting as pickets on the periphery. The manoeuvring of ships, the exchange of sensor and status information and the coordination and control of weapons and aircraft—so that real threats are engaged and friendlies ignored—constitutes a formidable task, demanding rapid and reliable force communications and the continuous attention of ship and squadron staffs. Some measure of the problem can be obtained from the statistics of the area or volume of interest to the sea commander. It has been calculated that in Nelson's day the admiral in command of a battle fleet was tactically interested in an area of about 2,500 square miles, limited by his own horizon and that of his scouting frigates. Today the Task Force Commander is immediately concerned with a volume of interest comprising no fewer than 53,000,000 cubic miles, taking into account his radar, sonar, satellite and intelligence sources, and the speed of modern aircraft and weapons.

Beneath the web of command described above, there is therefore a hive of activity within the force, responding to orders and instruction and in turn generating directions concerning the operation of weapons and sensors and the launching and deployment of aircraft. Such activity will chiefly be focused in Operations Rooms, nowadays equipped with the tactical computers and Combat Direction Systems, and linked by data link, described in the previous chapter. These facilities greatly increase the speed at which contacts are reported and analysed. As we have seen, the computers may propose specific operational responses, such as selecting the most appropriate weapon to engage an incoming threat. The controls enable each user to call up the information that he needs and to disregard irrelevant and distracting material. The overall effect is a dramatic improvement compared with earlier manually operated systems, not only in the rapidity of response but also the quality of decision-making. The work involved is highly skilled and dependent for its effectiveness on a sound understanding of the system and its underlying software. These skills are achieved only after training on specialised equipment, followed up by continual practice.

Command and Control of Naval and Maritime Aircraft

An extra dimension may be added to the command and control organisation by the need for special arrangements to deal with shore-based aircraft. This may take two forms. The first problem is encountered when air force units are operated in support of, and in conjunction with, naval units. This applies with particular effect in the United Kingdom, where the RAF provides all shore-based maritime aircraft and others, such as strike aircraft, committed to the maritime role. Service sensitivities require that resources are controlled by those who provide them; however sound and understandable this premise may be, it does lead to additional complexity in the command chain. Space allows only outline examination of the command structures involved. A naval commander-in-chief will have a senior but subordinate air force officer on his staff and under his operational command, sometimes known as the Air Deputy, who provides professional advice on the availability and employment of air force units. All such aircraft are under the full command of the air force commander-in-chief, who will assign maritime aircraft, and any other aircraft committed to the support of maritime operations, to the Air Deputy. The Air Deputy has command of the operational units so committed, as well as the relevant air bases and control rooms. The arrangement may sound somewhat unwieldy but works well in practice. It has the advantages that it gives the naval C-in-C operational command of maritime aircraft committed to the maritime role and provides him with the best professional advice on their use, while at the same time allowing the RAF to decide what aircraft are so committed, and then exercising operational control of them.

The provision of shore-based air support is a major concern of the naval command system. The planning and execution of sorties involves much activity at all levels. Task Force and Task Group Commanders may request support, such as anti-submarine surveillance patrols, anti-shipping reconnaissance and strike, or air cover when in suitable range of air bases. Alternatively the C-in-C or an Area Commander may initiate sorties without waiting for such requests from sea. When agreed, they are arranged by the air force officers on naval staffs, and the sorties are flown under air force operational control. Shore-based aircraft operating in direct support of naval units may, however, transfer to the control of such ships when in their immediate vicinity, provided that the ships are suitably equipped and have specialist direction staff. There is a great deal of signalling involved in the planning, mounting and execution of shore-based air support and the messages involved have been reduced to a series of formats. Each type of message (eg Request for Support; Aircraft Flight Plan and so forth) is identified by a designator. This reduces the length of the message and ensures that all necessary information is included. The series is an excellent example of the advantages of pre-formatting communications when possible.

A different type of command and control problem may arise when embarked

PLATE 7.6   A striking view of the USS *America* preparing to land aircraft. The flag hoists at her signal yards warn ships in the vicinity of her intended movements. (*Courtesy NAVAL FORCES/ US DOD*)

naval aircraft are operated in an area which is normally the responsibility of a shore-based air commander. Typically, this may happen in the Norwegian Sea when NATO naval units, including carriers, (eg the Strike Fleet), under the operational command of SACLANT, pass into an ocean area which is part of the European Air Defence Region, which is under SACEUR's command. The avoidance of mutual interference caused by two separately controlled groups of aircraft sharing the same air space poses a severe problem, as can be seen from Figure 7.1. This is partly because of the large tactical area covered by the Strike Fleet, which for its own defence must provide air cover and exercise surveillance over hundreds of miles 'up threat', and partly because of the large numbers of air tracks involved. The aircraft embarked in a typical Strike Fleet operation will often outnumber the combined operational strengths of the air forces committed to SACEUR for that area. This exacerbates the problems facing local Sector Operations Centres, which are presented with a major increase in friendly air activity from a powerful but transient force committed to the priority of its own operations. There is no simple operational solution, since the area concerned

PLATE 7.7   An RAF NIMROD long range maritime patrol aircraft. Special command structures are needed to integrate RAF aircraft with naval forces for maritime operations. (*Courtesy British Aerospace*)

FIGURE 7.1   NATO Strike Fleet. Tactical Operations areas

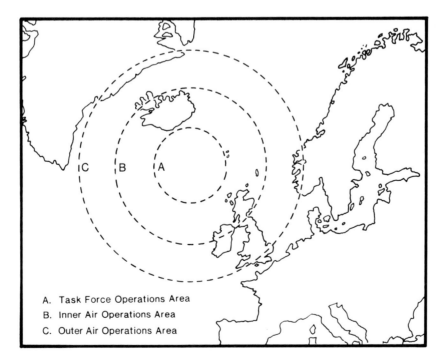

A. Task Force Operations Area
B. Inner Air Operations Area
C. Outer Air Operations Area

must clearly have a European-based air defence system which operates normally when the Strike Fleet is not in the Norwegian Sea; equally, NATO strategy requires SACLANT to deploy the Strike Fleet in the area when necessary. The problem can be reduced to manageable proportions by coordinating air operations, accomplished through the use of high-capacity data links for the rapid exchange of information, as described in the previous chapter. However, this cannot be said to be a completely satisfactory solution. The problem arises from the mobility of naval forces and a similar situation could occur anywhere where carrier-based air power is deployed into the area of interest of friendly shore-based air power.

Inshore Operations

A wide variety of naval tasks must be undertaken in coastal waters, in peace and war. In peace there is the need to patrol fishing grounds and otherwise police a country's offshore installations in the exclusive economic zone. There will be the need to conduct local exercises and trials within easy reach of bases. And there is the continual need to be able to react to maritime disasters and mount search and rescue operations. In war there will be the requirement to clear mines and maintain mine-free shipping lanes, to provide convoy routes and assembly anchorages, and to control merchant shipping and the entrances to ports. Most of these wartime tasks will be a continuing national responsibility and so directed through national command organisations, even in time of war; notable exceptions are the inshore operations conducted by Fast Patrol Boats in close waters such as the Baltic Approaches, which would be NATO operations of great importance.

Inshore operations tend to be of small scale and local in nature, involving single ships and small groups. The command system applied to them is usually based on the establishing of a series of contiguous coastal command areas, each with its own shore-based commander, whose chief responsibilities are the general direction and coordination of activity in the area, the promulgation of local information and intelligence, and control of shipping. At sea tactical command and control of each group will lie with the senior officer.

Amphibious Operations

The complexity of command and control reaches its zenith with amphibious operations, which will usually involve all the armed forces including—indeed especially—marines. Let us look first at a typical amphibious operation and then at the command arrangements. Let us assume that the aim of the operation is to land a sizable ground force, with its supporting arms, on hostile territory and to establish a secure beach-head from which subsequent land operations may be mounted. The operation will be planned in three phases. Phase One will be the Approach Phase, in which the specialised amphibious ships, with their helicopters and landing craft, and with ground troops and equipment on board, are escorted to the vicinity of the landing by the navy. A further convoy of 'ships taken up from trade' (STUFT) with heavy equipment, supplies and spares, and

PLATE 7.8   A broadside from the main armament of USS *Iowa*, the modernised United States battleship. Such firepower would provide invaluable naval gunfire support during an amphibious operation. (*Courtesy NAVAL FORCES/US DOD*)

possibly with requisitioned merchantmen acting as troopships for the second wave of army units, may be formed as a follow-up group. Phase One is an entirely naval phase, under naval command. Phase Two is the Assault Phase, in which the amphibious ships will land the army by helicopter and over the beach, supported by naval gunfire from ships and close support aircraft flown from the carriers. The Assault Group will, of course, be in the immediate vicinity of the beach-head and under an air defence umbrella provided by naval missile ships in close support and carrier-borne fighter aircraft. Command here is necessarily split, with control of the actual landings being exercised by the naval and army commanders of the assault group, with the main naval force lying off and acting in support as necessary. This is a critical time for command and control, covering the transition from naval to army primacy. Phase Three is when the beach-head is reasonably secure, and sufficient army units and equipment have been landed to enable the army commander to go ashore to take command of the land operation and establish his headquarters. Naval units will remain in support as requested by the army, and the build-up will continue, but the amphibious aspects of the operation are over as far as command and control are concerned.

It will be apparent that planning is crucial to the success of such an operation. Good planning is essential if the operation is to be mounted and executed smoothly; conversely, bad planning can be more deleterious to amphibious operations than any other activity of war, as the shambles of the landings at Gallipoli in World War I testify. The reader is referred to the sections on planning and command structure in Chapter 1, which apply with particular relevance.

The process must start with high level decisions on objectives, resources and timetables. Then there is the all-important matter of the command structure. This can be an emotive matter; unity and clarity of command is essential, but sensitivities towards placing control of men and resources under the command of another Service can cause problems which sometimes result in fudged arrangements. It should be the objective to place all units and resources committed to the operation under the command of one officer at the highest operational level. This will usually be the most appropriately placed Commander-in-Chief. If this is not done and, for instance, two Cs-in-C are involved, sooner or later the MOD may have to exercise its responsibility as the highest military authority to resolve differences, a cumbersome and far from ideal arrangement. In the case of the United Kingdom, responsibility for national operations outside the NATO area rests with Commander-in-Chief Fleet. For the Falklands Campaign, for example, he was designated as the overall commander of the operation and responsible for all the mounting and planning. He had a senior Army officer appointed as his Land Deputy, who took charge of land aspects of mounting and planning. The Royal Air Force felt it necessary for control of air force units, other than maritime aircraft, to remain under the command of Commander-in-Chief Strike Command, who operated in support of C-in-C Fleet. In the event, air force activity was mostly directed towards arranging and controlling the air lift to Ascension Island, so this potentially divisive organisation did not cause major problems.

At the Task Force level, command organisation is also highly involved, because of the tri-Service nature of the operation. The structures and procedures are generally well understood and frequently exercised. Smooth working is, however, dependent on good personal and professional relationships at commander and staff level, where the mix of Services is most apparent. Naval units will be organised and controlled much as for normal naval operations. The Assault Group will have permanently appointed naval and army commanders, who will be well practised in the unusual procedures involved in a landing operation, during which overall control passes from the Navy to the Army. There is a heavy dependence on communications planning, as the communications required for an amphibious landing are probably the most comprehensive of all. Normal naval communications are required throughout by the Task Force. Once the Army is ashore, it will need its own communications. In addition, during the actual assault and early build-up, communications must provide for the control of loading, deployment and turn round of landing craft and helicopters; requests for, allocation and control of gunfire and close support by aircraft; command liaison between the naval commander in the HQ ship and his army colleague as he moves ashore; and many other abnormal needs.

The concepts and procedures of modern amphibious operations stem from World War II, and the Combined Operations organisation established in the United Kingdom under Admiral Mountbatten and by the Americans for the planning and execution of their large-scale operations in the Pacific. The latter, in particular, set the pattern for the inter-service procedures involved in the effective mounting, execution and logistics support of what is the most complex of all military activities. Many authorities believe that the capacity to carry out successful amphibious operations represents the highest level of military achievement. It certainly involves all the arts discussed in this book.

Submarine Operations

Submarines are capable of performing a wide variety of operational tasks. Depending on the type of submarine and its armament, such tasks include the SLBM nuclear deterrent, hunter-killer operations against ships and other submarines, anti-submarine patrols and operations in direct support of surface ships, intelligence gathering and clandestine operations off enemy coasts. For all such tasks the submarine relies on its unique ability to remain undetected when submerged. The hunter-killer can present a hidden threat over wide areas of ocean and then achieve tactical surprise in attack; patrolling submarines can gather intelligence or detect passing targets without revealing their presence; and the submarine armed with strategic nuclear missiles can maintain an invulnerable second strike threat. The ability of the modern submarine to remain submerged and undetected is largely unimpeded. Nuclear-powered boats can operate fully submerged throughout their patrol, being virtually independent of the surface. Diesel-electric submarines no longer have to surface to charge batteries at night; this is done at periscope depth using the air breathing tube or snorkel. The risk of snorkel detection is small and precautions can be taken to minimise it.

As far as possible, therefore, command and control must be exercised without increasing the risks of submarine detection or inhibiting the submarine captain's freedom of manoeuvre. However, this is not easy to achieve since the physical phenomena which hide the submarine when submerged also make communicating with it very difficult (as explained in Chapter 5). Most modes of communicating with a submerged submarine require it to manoeuvre in a particular way, or expose it to possible detection in one form or another. Submarine command and control, and its associated communications, therefore require very careful planning, to reduce the need for signalling to the minimum and allow the captain tactical flexibility. It is based on the principle that the submarine captain is given his orders, kept informed on tactical developments in his area and then, as far as possible, left to get on with the job. His orders will be comprehensive and probably cast in the form of an Operation Order on the lines described in Chapter 1. Subsequent instructions on the method of execution will, if necessary, rely on the Rules of Engagement discussed earlier in this chapter; as we have seen these can be changed as required with minimum signalling.

In peace and war, a dived submarine is in a hazardous high-presure environment, constantly at risk to material failure or collision. Submarine safety is a continuing concern to everyone in the chain of command. To avoid mutual interference and to have some knowledge of submarines' whereabouts, the theatre of operations is divided into Submarine Operating Areas. Every submarine at sea is allocated exclusively one or more areas by his operating authority. Submarines must remain within their own allocated areas, which are changed as required for deployment and disposition. This method of separating submarines has tactical as well as safety advantages. A submarine detecting another submarine knows that it is not one of his force.

A further safety procedure is used to confirm that a submarine has surfaced safely after a period dived. The submarine originates a Diving Signal before submerging, giving its operational area and the time it intends to surface. On doing so, it makes a further short, high precedence signal, identifying itself and stating 'Surfaced'. Non-receipt of this signal by the time due would lead its operating authority to alert the well-proven submarine search-and-rescue organisation 'SUBMISS'. For a long patrol, the diving signal may cover the whole duration: if and when the submarine surfaces briefly during patrol it may originate a simple 'Check' signal, showing it is safe at that time. In war or emergency, the diving signal procedure may be amended or put in abeyance to avoid exposing the submarine to enemy detection from radio intercept and D/F.

The demanding nature of submarine operations causes most navies with such vessels to place their command in the hands of specialists. In the case of the Royal Navy all operational submarines are commanded by Flag Officer, Submarines (FOSM), who also administers them and directs their peacetime employment. In wartime FOSM, under the NATO command structure, would become Commander Submarines, Eastern Atlantic (COMSUBEASTLANT) and take operational command of all Allied submarines in that area. Unlike surface forces, with their subordinate structures of area and seagoing command, there is no need for a complex hierarchy for submarines. Direct operational control from one central authority who has all the necessary information to hand is the most efficient method.

The organisation and procedures described above are designed to provide the framework of submarine command and control with minimal communication. What signalling is needed is mostly from the command ashore to the submarine; reporting in from the boat is reduced to the minimum and may be eliminated altogether. However, it must be possible for the Command, both ashore and in the submarine, to follow and report the situation as it develops and to react to events as they occur. For this, real time communication is needed; however no method of communicating with submerged submarines is free from problems. As we have seen in Chapter 5, reception by the submarine of signal traffic, whether by VLF or satellite communications, necessitates it coming shallow, which restricts its tactical freedom and may mean breaking off a sonar contact. The use of reception from towed buoys is rather less restrictive, but confines the submarine's speed and depth within narrow limits. Transmission by submarine on HF is tantamount to announcing its position, given the efficiency of modern HFDF systems. Transmission and reception by satellite communications is rapid and carries much lower risk, but here again it entails coming shallow to periscope depth. Only transmission using expendable buoys enables the submarine to report to the shore command without operational penalty, and here the number of buoys is limited. To summarise, traditional methods such as VLF, combined with modern improvements such as satcom and buoys now provide a wide choice of communication mode. However, two-way communication with the shore is still inconsistent with the submarine having unrestricted choice of depth, course and speed, which it needs to preserve its security and perform its mission. The dilemma facing all submarine commanders, ashore and afloat, is the requirement to balance the need to communicate with the need to execute the task.

THE EXERCISE OF COMMAND

This book has examined the impact of modern technology on a subject that is close to the heart of all naval officers—command. We have seen how machines, whether they are radars, sonars, communications systems or computers, have transformed how the command of ships, weapons and men is exercised. There remains one question to be answered; how has this increasingly mechanical environment affected the personal relationships between senior and junior upon which command has relied so much in the past?

It would be easy to imagine that the darkened, computer-ridden atmosphere of an Operations Room would kill personal contact and that men would become mere extensions of the semi-intelligent machines they operate. This in fact is not the case; the greater the understanding of the computer, and its powers and limitations, the greater the appreciation of how the man in charge of it is thinking and why he is acting as he is. Personality and willpower can be projected just as much by the use of the computer (particularly if the user really understands what makes it work) as it can be by use of the telephone or signal pad. In any event, the commander will not spend all his time at his tactical console; at sea he will still spend many of his waking hours with his staff, and in harbour with those under his command. There is therefore still a need in the modern age, indeed an even greater one, for those qualities traditionally associated with the successful exercise of command. The setting of example, good judgement, a willingness to delegate and decisiveness—these and other personal attributes are what make the successful commander as much as his ability to understand and use computers, important though that has become.

What, however, will shine through all that the commander does will be his power of leadership. Whatever his rank or position, he must apply his authority in the direction of affairs, but the process can be accomplished only through subordinates and those lower in the chain. Although formal authority is necessary, it is rarely enough by itself; obedience that is given willingly and with respect for the superior will always be more effective. Leadership will inspire effort and engender morale, it will illuminate events and pluck success from the threat of failure. And the reputation of a great leader will go before him. This is not the place for an examination in depth of the qualities of leadership, nor to surmise how they can best be developed. At the risk of over-simplification, however, one can suggest that there are some recognisable characteristics which are common to most good leaders. Strong personality, coupled with self-confidence and sincerity are certainly essential ingredients, as is a genuine concern and interest in those who are led. Personal qualities by themselves, however, are not enough. They must be complemented by self-evident professional competence. Such qualities will show well enough, be their owner on the Bridge, in the Operations Room, or commanding the fleet from his Shore Headquarters.

8

The Way Ahead

THE earlier chapters of this book have described the operational procedures and supporting technology of naval command and control today. We will now explore how these may change during the next decade or two. Let us first look at what is likely to influence the process.

For the past fifty years, the chief engine of advance in military technology has been the combination of the scientist and operational expert, be he sailor, airman or soldier. They perform a closed loop function in which the sailor says what he wants from technology, and the scientist says what he can provide and how much it will cost. The sailor then amends his demands to a more realistic level, and the process continues until finance departments and politicians are prepared to endorse the procurement of tightly specified equipment. Research objectives, staff targets and staff requirements represent the formal stages of codifying the process and the whole procedure is subjected to close financial control and project management. In the early stages of a project, the 'sailor' will be the naval officer, fresh from sea and with innovative ideas, in the Operational Requirement (OR) directorate of his MOD. Later in the project, his role will be taken over by his counterpart the Application Officer, again a naval officer with recent operational experience, who will work closely with the scientists and engineers in the Research and Development Establishment; his job is to ensure that the equipment can be operated and maintained effectively in service.

One important evolutionary change in this process is already underway. During World War II and immediately after, the design and development of new equipment was necessarily performed in government laboratories and research establishments: industry manufactured the equipment to the resulting specification but, in the early years, lacked the capability of contributing to the design process. In the course of time, as industrial capability has grown, this division of functions has been eroded to the point where, in most Western nations with defence industries, government laboratories only carry out basic research and top secret development work and leave the remainder to industry. Government remains responsible for deciding the overall pattern of its procurement programme and deciding on detailed specifications of equipment and systems; its management of procurement is largely by means of contractual relationships, including tight control of quality and delivery. This involvement of industry has many advantages, which include the more effective harnessing of industrial R&D, better access to the innovative ideas of commerce, and wider markets for defence products. The increasing involvement of industry in the upstream end of defence procurement has led in the case of UK naval procurement to a change in the traditional Staff Requirement process. In recent years the RN has introduced a more flexible procedure in which only the general characteristics of the envisaged system are described in a 'Cardinal Point Specification' (CPS). This enables manufacturers to shape their proposals to MODs around their own products, exploiting their specialised skills and capabilities.

Sharing the initiative for equipment design between government and industry is also having other important effects on both the process and the product. One way of containing the insidious rise in defence equipment costs is to arrange larger volume production. Gone are the days when the smaller navies could afford to design and procure equipment in small quantities to meet their special needs; the fixed costs of development and production start-up must be spread over as many units as possible, preferably measured in hundreds. In the Western Alliance only the United States Navy has the size of fleet which requires equipments in such numbers. Increasingly, therefore, other navies must either buy American or collaborate to procure common equipment. Although much advanced military equipment will continue to be American in origin, international collaboration, particularly amongst European industry, is increasingly likely to become the chosen route for large and expensive systems beyond the capacity of national procurement programmes. Industrial cooperation leads to larger markets and the more effective integration of industrial capabilities. The process needs taut and complex management if costs are to be contained and delays avoided. But for many products—in particular those so large and expensive to be outside the reach of smaller nations—international industrial collaboration is the only practicable alternative to buying off-the-shelf.

Close industrial involvement in the procurement process may well offer other benefits to navies. For example, much military equipment nowadays has a natural commonality with its civil counterpart. This applies with particular force to communications and information processing systems, in which most of the

Plate 8.1   A US Navy air-cushion landing craft. This high-speed over-the-beach amphibious vessel represents naval technology on the move. (*Courtesy NAVAL FORCES/Bell Aerospace*)

basic functions are identical. In many cases, the military features that are required can be designed as additional rather than structural elements. Industry is therefore well placed to develop information technology to meet the needs of both civil and military users; this will lead to only one set of R&D costs and a wider market. The defence industry in advanced nations is already highly export conscious, as few manufacturers outside the United States can afford to concentrate on their home markets only. Systems that are designed to meet both civil and military needs, and find export outlet to wider markets, will sell in far higher numbers than those aimed at the military home market only.

Contractual relationships with defence suppliers, based on solicited proposals in response to broad criteria such as the cardinal point specification already mentioned, could with benefit be used in other novel ways. For instance there is an increasing need for effective but cheaper equipment, of lower absolute cost, rather than more expensive equipment of greater capability. This could be represented in the CPS as a feature with high weighting in bid assessment, so encouraging innovative ideas from industry. Another approach to cost reduction could be to specify that tenders for the supply of equipment must include fixed price quotations for a maintenance contract, covering the first few years of system life. This would ensure that manufacturers had reliability and maintainability at heart during design, as much as performance and profit.

The evident need to contain defence costs has led to proposals for a more radical approach to defence programmes. It has come to be termed 'specialisation' whereby responsibility for specified major areas of defence equipment (eg surface warships; submarines; mine-countermeasures; tanks; combat aircraft) are divided between individual nations of the NATO Alliance, rather than undertaken by any or all as at present. This far-reaching concept is not new, but has never found favour, largely because of the effect it would have on national defence and industrial capabilities. It seems unlikely to attract sufficient political support in the near future.

Increasing industrial involvement nationally, and collaboration internationally is therefore the likely procurement scenario in which military equipment, especially that serving the command and control process, will be produced. At the beginning of this chapter it was suggested that, for many decades, the chief engine of advance in military technology has been the combination of the scientist and the operational expert. It is clear that this analogy now needs updating. The engine of change in future will be, as ever, the availability of technology coupled to the needs of the customer, but it will be more market oriented, and so more industrially led, than in the past. The challenge to governments will be to learn how to access and steer this process to their advantage, rather than run it directly.

It will be helpful to an understanding of how military capabilities evolve to recognise two complementary influences, which can be described as 'technology push' and 'operations pull'. Technology offers new capabilities to military policy makers. These will often meet perceived needs and be implemented on that basis. However, a further factor exists; new technology advances the potential state of the art, and—even if the resulting systems do not directly commend themselves as both operationally necessary and financially affordable—the fact that the enemy may acquire them must be taken into account. These two factors create a strong 'technology push' towards implementing state-of-the-art systems, although financial constraints will regulate the process. The converse of this process is the influence of the perceived need itself. Weaknesses in capability will be apparent to serving officers and their civilian colleagues, and create demand for new equipment with better performance. This will direct R&D and, if technology can provide the required performance at affordable cost, will result in new equipment. This is 'operations pull'; it represents customer demand, which industry is always out to discover and satisfy; however, meeting the demand is dependent on science being able to produce the required answer, which is not always the case. Later in this chapter we shall discuss some examples of perceived military need which are likely to remain unsatisfied for some time at least.

An example of how equipment design can advance without the impetus of 'operations pull', but still offer useful military capabilities as part of 'technology push', is the increasing tendency in the electronics industry to manufacture products conceived and designed as large systems. In this context, a system can be defined as the interconnection of a number of individual equipments so that they interoperate together as a functional whole. There are several reasons for

PLATE 8.2   A US Navy F/A 18 fighter/attack aircraft being readied for catapult launch. The effectiveness and mobility of carrier based airpower remains a potent force in world affairs. (*Courtesy NAVAL FORCES/McDonnell Douglas Corp.*)

this. It is now possible to integrate modern electronic equipment into complex but reliable systems, which provide a performance which could not be approached by attempting to operate the same equipment using manual methods. Indeed a system approach, based on digital processing, software integration and computer control, frequently offers the only practicable method of exploiting the available technology. Furthermore the removal of human interfaces achieves significant manpower savings, leading to greater reliability and consistency of operation, and lower life costs. The manufacturing costs of systems are often less than the alternative of making and marketing large numbers of individual equipments. Finally, the system approach solves what is otherwise left to the customer, the problems of interconnection; few customers these days wish to buy a set of disparate equipments and deal with integration and interoperability at their own expense and risk.

These trends are increasingly leading governments and other major customers to perceive that their requirements for equipment, again particularly in the field of communications and information technology, are best specified as complete working systems rather than sets of individual equipments to be acquired separately and then integrated. This will have a significant effect on the structure of industry; only the very largest companies have the technical capability and financial strength to seek business competitively for such major products. Other companies will find themselves forced either to merge to form such units, or act as sub-contractors to the system suppliers. There will therefore be fewer suppliers, fewer products and less choice. The process will, in some ways, ameliorate one of the more intractable problems of modern technology, inter-operability, since equipment forming part of a system will of course interoperate throughout its domain. However the lack of choice will mean that the special needs of customers like navies may not be met unless they or their governments have been involved at the conceptual and design stages. Since many communications oriented systems will be international in nature this is a further factor impelling both governments and industries to collaborate internationally.

A number of technical developments are influencing the trend towards systems. One is the well-known growth in the capability of silicon chip implanted circuitry. Probably of equal significance, although less in the public eye, is the increasing use of digital signal processing as the basis of equipment design. Most people will be familiar with analogue equipment, that is individual 'black boxes' which function in one mode only, for which their components, such as resistors, capacitors and transistors, have been selected and connected. Such black boxes then function as filters, detectors, amplifiers and the like, and are interconnected to form complete equipments such as receivers, transmitters and modems. Digital signal processing (DSP) replaces this network of inflexible analogue components with a basic equipment formed from simple logical circuits. This processes the information in digital form to provide inputs and outputs corresponding to the analogue equivalent. The real significance of the technique is that the internal configuration of the device, which determines its function, is organised by the use of appropriate control signals, ie the program or software. This means that a small number of DSP devices can be used under software control to provide, sequentially, the whole range of functions required for an analogue equipment. For example DSP circuits could be changed from performing a filter function, to an amplification function and thence to a detector function, to provide the equivalent of a receiver front end. The effect is that equipments and systems can be composed of large numbers of standard devices, the functions and interconnection of which will be determined by software.

The versatility of DSP described in the previous paragraph applies in similar fashion to any digital equipment, in contrast to the inherent inflexibility of analogue equipment. In the latter the physical and electrical characteristics of the various components used to create the equipment are fixed. This tends to freeze not only the function for which the equipment has been designed but also establishes, in unchanging form, the parameters of its inputs and outputs. Interconnection of two such equipments, unless the input of one corresponds with the output of the other, can be effected only by interposing between them an interface device, whose inputs and outputs do correspond and thus enable the three to interoperate. The only way to avoid the need for interface devices is to design equipment to common technical standards which render them compatible. International standards are being advanced all the time, and provide the means by which civil systems can be designed and operated in compatible fashion world-wide; the problem with many military systems is that, being 'state-of-the-art', they will be introduced into service before their associated standards have been agreed and implemented. There is also the problem of interconnecting 'old and new', which was discussed in an earlier chapter. The great advantage of digitally based equipment is that it is far easier to arrange that inputs and outputs are compatible, or if not so, to provide a relatively simple interface device. The chief component of inputs and outputs of any equipment is the way in which information is expressed—in analogue equipment by means of analogue signals such as the value of a voltage or frequency, in digital equipment by means of the coding of a stream of bits. Thus, with digital equipment, inter-connectivity is largely a matter of software, which is more flexible and amenable to change than existing and immutable hardware.

The flexibility of configuration conferred by digital signal processing can also be used to create more versatile equipment, sometimes known as 'multi-functional'. We have already alluded in a previous chapter to an early type, the phased array radar, in which beam scanning is effected by electrical means rather than the physical rotation and elevation of a conventional aerial. It will be appreciated how this can be accomplished technically from what has been said about DSP. This principle can be taken much further. If the functions performed by the sub-units of an equipment can be altered rapidly and at will there is no reason to limit the function of the whole equipment to a role which has to date been imposed by the restrictions and inflexibility of analogue techniques. In theory, at least, radars could have an ESM mode, so that the receiving chain could alternate between reception of the radar echo and broader band scanning for interception of enemy radars etc. The multi-functional nature of such an equipment could be further extended by making the radar transmitter double as a versatile ECM device, the mode of transmission being timed-shared between the two roles as required. Versatility can also be achieved through 'modularity',

PLATE 8.3   A squadron of NATO Tripartite minesweepers deploy for operations. Surface warships are essential for many naval tasks in peace and war. (*Courtesy NAVAL FORCES/Audio Visuele Dienst KM*)

that is the ability to change an equipment's function or performance by changing or adding whole modules, such as an extra power amplifier.

So far the main thrust of this chapter has been a discussion of the likely availability of new and relevant technology, developed by industry for the civil market, but where appropriate and with suitable adaptation used by the armed forces for military purposes. We have called this process 'technology push'. The other influence at work, which we have called 'operations pull', in which gaps in military capability are identified as requirements, with the intention of satisfying them by directing government funded R&D, or by encouraging industry to deploy R&D resources at a military market. Let us look at some of the directions in which this latter process is likely to operate in the next few years.

If one asked a senior naval officer what he considered to be the greatest threat to his ability to exercise command and control in war his reply would probably reflect his concern that the communications available in peace would be taken out by the enemy at the opening stages of hostilities. The threats relate chiefly to the vulnerability of satellites and the exposure of tactical radio circuits to enemy ECM at the critical moment of attack. Let us first examine the latter of these concerns. The antidotes to enemy jamming of radio communications have been discussed in general terms in Chapter 3; two approaches were identified— frequency agility, or frequency hopping; and the use of spread spectrum. The extent to which techniques such as these are likely to feature in civil systems in future is not yet clear. On the one hand they introduce expense and some loss of capacity, possibly for little civil advantage. On the other, the need for security in civil systems is growing; in addition, such techniques as spread spectrum could offer a means of reliable performance in harsh radio environments, and thus justify their extra cost. Whatever the outcome for civil use they are certainly high in defence equipment shopping lists. The term used to describe the general capability of circuits protected by such techniques is 'ECM resistance'. One important new system, JTIDS, discussed at some length earlier in this book, is already in service in AWACS aircraft and will probably be more widely deployed during the 1990s. Other systems, perhaps less complex, will probably follow. During the era under discussion the need to render vital circuits ECM-resistant is likely to become a recognised feature of naval command and control, in much the same way as today it is normal to provide such circuits with on-line cryptographic or speech secrecy protection.

The other concern, satellite vulnerability, is less amenable to solution. Satellites can be taken out by physical attack, by high level nuclear explosions and probably in future by laser weapons. They are also prone to catastrophic failure and, as events in the last few years have shown, highly exposed to the deleterious effects of gross interruption of the availability of launch vehicles. Satellites provide the backbone of the world-wide command and control system of the Western Alliance. It must be feared that, potentially at least, they also represent its Achilles' heel. Perhaps one of the most pressing military needs at the moment is a fall-back system which could cope in adequate degree if the worst happened. Modern techniques could be used to enhance the reach and reliability of High Frequency for this purpose, and there is some evidence that such techniques, for so long apparently ignored by the military and scientific

PLATE 8.4   USS *Alabama* (SSBN 731). The ability of the nuclear-powered submarine armed with strategic missiles to pose an invulnerable second strike deterrent is unlikely to be diminished. (*Courtesy NAVAL FORCES/General Dynamics*)

community, are at last beginning to attract attention. If so, during the next decade or two we may see the ionosphere, a natural phenomenon which is continuously in orbit, and available without charge, being used to underpin satellites for long-distance communications.

There will be other fields in which naval officers would like science to wave a wand, but where magical solutions will not be forthcoming. One is likely to be progress in underwater sensors. Despite the vast sums spent on underwater research, basic physics appear to be against the chances of extending the use of electromagnetic waves below the surface of the sea. The exceptions will remain, largely as they are today, the marginal incursions of VLF and ELF waves—which cannot be used for detection—and the limited degree of penetration achievable by high-power lasers. These minor improvements, and others that may be obtained from research in related fields—such as the detection by infra-red sensors of wakes and effluents—are unlikely to amount to the sort of break-through that would expand what we have termed the electromagnetic environ-ment to embrace the submarine world. The submarine is therefore likely to retain its chief characteristic and operational advantage, namely the ability to remain hidden. However the corollary is inescapable: the laws that govern the propagation of EM waves and prevent the use of radar underwater apply with equal force to radio communication. Tomorrow's submarine will remain a most potent military instrument, and as such must come under positive command and control. The carefully designed methods we have examined in earlier chapters will remain both available and adequate for such purposes. The dilemma will nevertheless persist. To secure its objectives the submarine must remain sub-merged and undetected, with tactical freedom of manoeuvre; however when in its world deep beneath the waves it is, outside its own local and limited environment, not only hidden but unhearing, and largely unhearable. The paradox is that by taking action to open communication with higher command the submarine may jeopardise its operational mission and hazard its own security.

The surface warship, with its ability to maintain continuous communications via radio and satellites, with reliable knowledge of its tactical area and local air space, and with room for computers, ops rooms and command facilities, will therefore remain the platform from which command and control of a force or local area is exercised. Of one thing we can be confident, there will be a continuing and growing requirement for tight control of naval forces, wherever they may be. We live in too dangerous a world for politicians to leave to the man in the front line, or at the scene of trouble, decisions on which the future of a government, or the issue of peace or war, could turn. This leads to an interesting conclusion. The world-wide span of command and control now makes it possible to bring navies under continuous high level direction: in circumstances of confrontation the actions of naval commanders will therefore be judged by the other side to be politically authorised. The requirement to provide such direction thus becomes paramount. Command and control creates its own imperative.

Self Test Questions

The questions, shown by chapters below, are designed to help the student. They have been so framed that the answers may be found without difficulty within the text of the appropriate chapter.

Chapter 1

1.1   By what authority do naval officers exercise command?

1.2   Why is it sometimes appropriate for the senior officer of a naval force to delegate command to a subordinate, and how would this be effected?

1.3   How does the designation of the commander of an operational unit in a Task Organisation denote his place in the command hierarchy?

1.4   How and when are national forces assigned to NATO Command in a war emergency?

1.5   What is meant if an officer is said to 'wear two hats' and what advantages can stem from this procedure?

1.6   How will a commander-in-chief receive political direction on his operational objectives?

1.7   What are the main elements of an Operation Order?

1.8   Why is the existence of common doctrine important in the direction of naval operations?

1.9   Why do commanders-in-chief nowadays exercise command and control from shore headquarters rather than a flagship?

1.10   Distinguish between 'tactics' and 'tactical command and control'.

Chapter 2

2.1   In what frequency bands do most modern ship and aircraft surveillance radars operate, and why?

2.2   What is meant by 'anaprop' and why is it difficult to make operational use of this phenomenon?

2.3   What is meant by the description '3-D radar' and what operational advantages do such equipments have over conventional radars?

2.4   Why is AEW coverage important to a force commander?

2.5   Why must IFF transmissions be encrypted?

2.6   What are the required characteristics of a navigation radar?

2.7   Why is ESM a valuable adjunct to surveillance radar?

2.8   Why are the capabilities provided by radio navigation systems useful to naval command and control?

2.9   How is the information obtained from satellite surveillance analysed and correlated?

2.10   How has the advent of satellite surveillance affected the command and control of naval forces?

Chapter 3

3.1   What are the two distinct operational effects to which ECM techniques may be applied?

3.2   Why may it be dangerous to use noise jamming against incoming missiles?

3.3   Why are some types of ECM best used as shock tactics, and what operational effects will be aimed at?

3.4   Why must ships manoeuvre when using off-board decoys as anti-missile protection?

3.5   What features of a warship are likely to be used as a target by an infra-red homing missile?

3.7   Why will ESM often provide the first indication of an enemy's approach?

3.8   How is the techique known as reciprocal intercept used to assist submarines?

3.9   What is the best means of preventing an enemy practising ECM or ESM against you?

3.10   Why must the EMCON policy of a force at sea be kept continuously under review?

Chapter 4

4.1   What causes cavitation, and how does this phenomenon affect sonar performance and design?

4.2   How does the temperature gradient of the sea affect sound propagation, and how do ships obtain local knowledge of it?

4.3   Why cannot underwater surveillance provide tactical information of comparable quality to that available from above water surveillance?

4.4   How does a submarine captain use his knowledge of local temperature conditions to obtain tactical advantage over enemy warships?

4.5   What types of sonar are designed to be towed astern, and what advantages are thus obtained compared with hull-mounted equipments?

4.6   By what means may fixed wing aircraft and helicopters detect submarines?

4.7   What are the advantages of the use of passive, as opposed to active, sonar?

4.8   In what positions are bottom-mounted sonars likely to be sited, and for what purpose?

4.9   Why are ships fitted with towed arrays usually stationed well clear of the main force?

4.10   Why will a submarine intending to attack surface ships attempt to approach at low speed?

Chapter 5

5.1   In what ways does a naval signal differ from a telex?

5.2   In naval parlance what is the difference in meaning between 'propose' and 'intend'?

5.3   What advantages are obtained by using multi-frequency techniques for the operation of long-range HF broadcast and ship-shore services?

5.4   What are the approximate limits of coverage of a geo-stationary communications satellite stationed on the Greenwich meridian?

5.5   What band of frequencies provides the majority of line-of-sight radio circuits in a naval task force, and for what purposes will such circuits be used?

5.6   What constraints on the setting-up and interconnection of ships communication equipment to meet the ship's COMPLAN will restrict the Communications Officer's freedom of choice?

5.7   What factors tend to militate against the provision of a satisfactory level of communications interoperability amongst NATO navies?

5.8   How is a VLF broadcast conducted so that a submarine captain can choose the time to receive his message traffic, and why is this important to submarine operations?

5.9   What is the difference between on-line and off-line cryptographic systems, and why is the former to be preferred for the protection of naval communications circuits?

5.10   What modern technical features and other improvements have made naval communications more reliable than in the past?

Chapter 6

6.1   Why was it necessary for the Captain to move from the Bridge to the Operations Room, as the place from which to take charge of the fighting of the ship?

6.2   How do the controls of a tactical console enable a user to view only those features of immediate concern to him?

6.3   Why is an automatic weapon response to sea skimming missiles a necessary form of defence against such threats?

6.4   What advantages does a Distributed Combat Direction System have over a Centralised Combat Direction System?

6.5   Why is it necessary for data link message standards to be agreed internationally and in such fine detail?

6.6   Why is it difficult to develop tracks from targets reported by data link, and in what way will the introduction of GPS ameliorate this?

6.7   What NATO data link enables non-computer fitted ships to have access to selected information from ships in the force fitted with tactical ADP systems?

6.8   How do the functions performed by shore based computer systems, as installed in naval shore headquarters, differ from those performed by tactical systems in ships?

6.9   What advantages, as compared with manual methods, can computers offer in naval command and control?

6.10   Why is software such an intrusive and important constituent of naval command and control, and what responsibilities do naval commanders and their staffs have towards the software in their ships and weapons?

Chapter 7

7.1   During a period of confrontation how will the captains of ships be kept informed of the circumstances in which they may open fire?

7.2   Why is it essential for admirals and captains at sea to have formal arrangements for deputies to relieve them when required?

7.3   What are the sources of the common doctrine which enables a NATO force to operate effectively immediately it is assembled?

7.4   Describe some of the operational tasks that, within the NATO Alliance, will remain a national responsibility in war.

7.5   If a naval commander-in-chief has an Air Deputy, what will be his responsibilities and functions?

7.6   Why will the movement of a carrier task force into a sea area, the air space of which is under the control of a shore-based air commander, create operational difficulties and how can these best be mitigated?

7.7   Why does the Assault Phase of an amphibious operation create special problems for command and control?

7.8   What method is used to separate submarines during operational deployment, and why does this have tactical as well as safety advantages?

7.9   What would happen if a submarine failed to pass its surfacing signal to its operational commander ashore by the time it was due?

7.10   Why, in an age when command and control is increasingly conducted via computers, do personal relationships and qualities traditionally associated with leadership remain essential constituents of the exercise of command?

Chapter 8

8.1   How do the naval officer and the scientist co-operate to design and develop new naval equipment, and how is this process now evolving?

8.2   What advantages to naval equipment procurement stem from an increasing involvement with industry in the conceptual and design stages?

8.3   What factors influence the trend towards equipment increasingly being designed and manufactured as components of large systems?

8.4   Why are we likely to see an increasing use of international industrial collaboration as a method of procurement?

8.5   What advantages to equipment design can be obtained from the use of digital signal processing techiques?

8.6   What is meant by 'multi-functional' systems and what advantages do such equipment offer navies?

8.7   What techniques are likely to be used to provide communications systems with ECM resistance?

8.8   Why does the book suggest that satellite communications are both the backbone and the Achilles' heel of command and control, and what is proposed to ameliorate the latter?

8.9   Why is the surface ship likely to remain the platform from which command and control of a force or local area is exercised?

8.10   The book suggests that 'command and control creates its own imperative'. Discuss.

About the Author

Captain Pakenham served for 35 years in the Royal Navy as a Seaman Officer. His senior appointments included Assistant Director of Naval Plans in the Ministry of Defence, Director of Naval Signals and Chief Naval Signal Officer, and Director of the Royal Naval Staff College, Greenwich.

On retirement in 1979 he established himself as a Naval Consultant; he is currently adviser on naval applications and requirements to the Racal Electronics Group. His series of articles on 'The Command and Control of Naval Operations' is being published in the defence magazine *NAVAL FORCES*.

THE CO-AUTHORS

After an extensive career in naval weapons research and development in the Ministry of Defence, *Dr D. G. Kiely* retired as The Head of Profession in naval weapons, and The Chief Naval Weapon Systems Engineer. He introduced the Cardinal Points method of weapons procurement, and has published a number of contributions in the weapons field.

R. E. Legate has worked in the field of ASW technology since 1957. He was appointed Chief Engineer of Plessey Marine Systems Division on its formation in 1961, and in that position was responsible for the industrial contribution to a number of Royal Navy ASW equipments. He is now retired but continues to work as a consultant to Plessey Naval Systems.

Captain David Whitehead served in the Royal Navy for 35 years, 25 of them as a communications specialist. As well as three sea commands, he held senior C^3 appointments in both the Ministry of Defence in London, and in the Pentagon. He is now a director in the Racal Electronics Group.

Index